I0058160

LEADING WITH
CHARACTER

Mastering the Habits of Highly Successful Business Leaders

BY SUZAN HART

© 2013 SUZAN HART. ALL RIGHTS RESERVED

ALL RIGHTS RESERVED. NO PART OF THIS WORK MAY BE REPRODUCED OR STORED IN AN INFORMATIONAL RETRIEVAL SYSTEM, WITHOUT THE EXPRESS PERMISSION OF THE PUBLISHER IN WRITING.

FOREWORD BY KATHY COOVER
COVER DESIGN BY PETER AINLEY
PHOTO OF SUZAN BY MARYLYN LINGE

ISBN1927677556

Dedication

With much gratitude,
I dedicate this book to my **mother Lorna Gordon**.
You are truly a leader and a visionary. Thank you for
showing me that all I desire is truly possible.

Cindy Salter, thank you for your gift of friendship.
Your encouragement, faith and support have helped
all my dreams become a reality.

Osei, Francis and PJ, thank you for being
such blessings in my life.

ACKNOWLEDGEMENTS

Thank you to:

- Jim and Kathy Coover for the opportunity to dream and learn to live my life on purpose.
- Shannon O'Neil, for always finding a solution and going above and beyond. You are the best assistant anyone could ask for.
- Mr. Don Caldwell for setting the bar high and teaching me self mastery.
- Cheri Elder, who taught me that my best could always get better.
- Joy Lepage for your continued example of integrity.
- Susan Sly for being bold, setting the pace and believing we could have it all.
- Angela Robertson for your confidence. You helped me heal, risk, grow and trust my intuition.
- David Wood for helping find my true voice.
- Dr. Tony O'Donnell for your continued encouragement
- Matt Rockwell for your wisdom and insight.

CONTENTS

FOREWORD

Leading With Character is a well-thought-out, deep, purposeful book.

I have had the privilege of watching Suzan Hart grow and develop as a leader over the past nine years. This book truly comes from her journey. Suzan understands that the first person we each lead is ourselves, and it is only then that we truly step into leadership and influence others. This book brilliantly reveals equations that capture the essence of the twenty habits of successful business leaders.

As I read the manuscript for *Leading With Character*, I realized that everyone can get value from this book. If you are searching for clarity and face challenges with your leadership, this book is for you. If you are already successful, you will find within the pages a well-laid-out tool to bring your leadership to the next level.

I don't have to work another day in my life, yet I continue to strive for more. I have a large vision and I love what I do. I strive for more because I want others to have success and have the opportunity to contribute to something larger than themselves. This book is a clear tool I can use on this journey. As I have grown as a leader over the years, I have learned that it is an ongoing process of always working on self. This book will give you the tools to honor your word and stand by your commitments.

Suzan is an excellent communicator. She has a way of expressing herself that will move you and touch your heart. Suzan has nailed the definitions of each habit by using word equations and personal stories to paint a picture that will give you a deeper explanation and empower you to take clear action

Leading With Character is like a John C. Maxwell book; you will go back to it time and time again. Suzan has laid out a step-by-step simple read that is easy to understand. She has put deep thought into every chapter, creating a guide to help everyone develop their leadership capacity.

I encourage you to read through *Leading With Character* once. Then read the book again, focusing on a chapter each month. Do the exercises, as each habit will come to fruition when you answer the questions and take the appropriate action. Nothing is easy in life. Success takes time, and success takes leadership. *Leading With Character* is a phenomenal read for those who have the courage to master the habits that build the character of successful leaders.

Kathy Coover

INTRODUCTION

How many of you have heard the quote "If you are leading and no one is following, then you're only taking a walk"? While having followers is a common determiner of leadership, I believe that having followers in and of itself does not truly define leadership. The real question is "Why are people following?" or "What has motivated people to follow?" Are they following from a place of inspiration, or are they following from a place of desperation?

According to Steven Covey (author of *The Seven Habits of Highly Effective People*), people often confuse leadership with management. To manage is to tell people what to do. It is to outline tasks, give instruction, set deadlines and manage a process. The right to manage is often granted because of position, title, or the power to withhold a desired or valued resource. In these cases, people follow because of a fear of loss or the possibility of exclusion. If this so-called "leader" were stripped of title and position, they might instantly lose followers. The right to lead most often requires no title; rather, it is often earned by how we consistently show up in the world.

This book is a product of my desire to truly lead: to develop the character that myself and others can trust and count on. Each idea is a reflection of part of my search for understanding and skills on my leadership journey. With this book, you will have the opportunity to explore practical habits that, when embodied, will enable you to continue to grow and enhance your leadership capacity and attract quality individuals to your team.

I am a black woman who was born on the small island of Trinidad. My family moved to Canada when I was five, and I was raised in a small town in the province of Quebec. Some would call me an African Canadian, while others would call me black, a visible minority, or a host of other descriptives. No matter what the title, as I grew up in Canada I soon learned the color or my skin was a source of discrimination, stereotyping and racism. I also learned I could believe the low expectations society at times had for those who looked like me, or I could walk to my own beat. Fortunately, I had a mother who had high expectations and gave little attention to the opinions of others. My quest for leadership was how my mother taught me to cope with racism. You see, leaders are defined by their character and individuals with great character consistently rise above the misconceptions that give racism and discrimination power. Learning to lead myself allowed me to develop independent thoughts, behaviors and actions. It taught me that consistency of habits and actions eventually determined how people chose to treat me. I trust this book will remind anyone who is faced with discrimination, stereotypes and bias to rise above the chatter and take the lead in defining his or her life.

The habits described in this book were also practiced on my journey to become a full-time professional network marketer. What this means is I earn my income by marketing a product or service through the process of building and leading a network of people who do the same. When people think of network marketing, they usually identify the first part: marketing or selling a product or service. In my opinion, the most powerful part is building and leading an effective network, and that part is not often talked about. It is often confused with hunting down and convincing friends and family to join you. However, the development of great leadership skills is what can separate an average networker from a great network marketer.

Great network marketers are some of the best leaders I have encountered. They are among a select group of people who have mastered the art of leadership and attracting inspired followers. They are leading a network of people who come not because of the guarantee of a pay cheque; rather, they come because they are inspired by a common vision and voluntarily follow. They willingly follow because they have connected with a leader's belief in what is possible, and they stay when the actions the leader models have them believe the result they are seeking is truly possible. Caught up in the right leadership environment, these followers are willing to be unreasonable and to push past challenges to achieve a common goal. Martin Luther King's speech "I Have a Dream" is a perfect example of how one man's vision followed by focused action can inspire a nation to act. The speech inspired people to be unreasonable, and, in many cases, risk their personal and psychological safety because they believed so much more was possible.

So what is leadership? I believe it is the ability to influence others. It is to inspire people to act because they choose to, not because they have to. To lead is the act of doing. It is to go first, to set the example and to be the cause of inspired action. It is to have a vision and behave in a manner that inspires others to act alongside you. It is to co-create other leaders. To truly understand leadership is to understand that the first person you will ever lead is yourself.

> *Sow an act, reap a habit*
> *Sow a habit, reap a character*
> *Sow a character, reap a destiny.*
> **-Anonymous**

So how do you lead yourself and become a person that people view as an effective leader? How do you develop the character of a leader? To answer this question is to understand a working definition of the word "character." One's character is sum total of your daily habits, executed over time. It is our automatic way of being. The things we say and the actions we take without conscious thought. The end result is we become known for what we habitually do, and that in turn shapes how we show up in the world, the life we design and the character we are known for.

Last year I had the privilege of coaching Laurie. Laurie had come to me because she had a desire to release about fifty pounds. She explained she had tried many diets and nothing seemed to work. Although Laurie knew what she needed to do, she was frustrated because she had no motivation to diet or exercise. Listening to Laurie, my first response was that her focus was in the wrong place. I explained to her that a diet was a destination, and the minute she arrived at her target weight loss she would stop the restrictive activity that created the results and then resume her past behaviors. Laurie admitted this was exactly what had occurred many times before. I explained to Laurie that her health today was a sum of poor habits in the area we can call health and nutrition. Her personal leadership in the area of health was ineffective. Permanent change would come not when she focused on weight loss, but when she focused on changing the habits that caused the byproducts of weight gain and poor health. The solution was to replace ineffective habits with habits that would permanently move her in the direction of good health. I explained to Laurie that, unlike a diet, changing habits is not a quick fix. It would take time and she would also experience periods of discomfort. Each negative habit would need to be replaced with a positive, effective habit. This process is like uprooting a large maple tree and replacing it with a small sapling. The sapling will not have the same strength or deep roots as the original maple.

Over the next six months, I watched Laurie begin to change her habits and lead herself in the area of health for the first time. During this journey we rarely spoke of Laurie's weight. Rather, we spoke about Laurie's habits around communication, expressing emotions, coping with stress, and planning her day. By developing some guiding principles and exploring habits like empowered communication, commitment, integrity and self-mastery, Laurie began scheduling time to work out, plan and prepare meals, and educate herself on healthy food choices. Laurie also learned how to express her emotions rather than stuff them with comfort food. She began to ask for what she desired and to set limits. As Laurie began to develop the character of a person committed to health, the ripple effect was that pounds and inches began to melt away. Although this did not occur as quickly as in a crash diet, Laurie feels the change is more permanent because she has created new habits. Interestingly, as Laurie began to lead herself around health, her family has also begun to follow.

This book is collection of some of the habits I believe form the character of great leaders. Creating mastery of many of these habits will not only impact your business;

the ripple effect will change every area of your life. The goal of this book is not to give you a dictionary definition of a word; the goal is to give you a description of the word that enables you to embody the word and create it as a functional, actionable part of your daily life.

Have you ever caught yourself using a word, yet you were unsure how to be that word in your life? You grasp the definition of the word, yet you are unsure of the actions that would enable you to embody the word and give it life in your world. You see, we often use words with little consideration to the behaviors or actions necessary to make that word come alive. Take the words "commitment" or "integrity." While I might understand the dictionary definition of either word, translating that word into actions that enable me to behave as a person with integrity or be an example of commitment may be more challenging.

I believe words paint pictures in our mind that are positive or negative, empowering or disempowering. Whether a word moves us forward pushes us backwards or keeps us in the same place is determined by the working definition we give it: the picture it paints in our mind. Our ability to embody a word in a manner that moves our life forward is totally determined by the picture we create in our mind and the actions that stem from that picture.

In this book I will share my working definition of twenty habits I believe can transform a person's life. As I define each habit, I encourage you to use my working definition or use my insight as a catalyst to define your own. The goal is to enable each of us to paint an empowering picture that evokes positive emotions and clear and powerful action. My desire is to create an awareness which allows each of us to sow the habits and reap the character of a leader.

Bonus 1: Before we begin our journey together, I encourage you to take a moment and go to www.lwcbook.com and complete the **Penthouse Leadership Assessment.** If you are committed to creating change, it is important to track your progress and course-correct as necessary. Doing the Penthouse Leadership Assessment will allow you to determine a beginning score for each habit. As you implement your plan designed to improve your mastery of each habit, you will be able to go back the Penthouse Leadership Assessment and track your progress.

Have fun and enjoy the journey!

awareness which allows each of us to know the habits and reap the charge and benefit.

Bonus - Before we begin our journey together, I encourage you to take a moment and go to www.[webitk].com and complete the Penthouse Leadership Assessment. If you are committed to creating change, it is important to track your progress and course-correct as necessary. Using the Penthouse Leadership Assessment will allow you to determine a beginning score for each habit. As you implement your plan designed to improve your mastery of each habit, you will be able to re-take the Penthouse Leadership Assessment and track your progress.

Have fun and enjoy the journey!

1. Commitment:

(Purpose + Focus + Action) x Time

> **When I make a decision,**
> **I do what is required.**

Interesting word, "commitment"... *Webster's Dictionary* defines commitment as an obligation. The root word, commit, means to be obligated; it is the act of binding yourself intellectually, physically and emotionally to a course of action. I love that: "binding yourself intellectually, physically and emotionally to a course of action." Commitment is an act of managing self, staying in the game and on the court till the end, to pursue something worthy and worthwhile until it is achieved. Strong leaders understand that the journey has many peaks and valleys. They are committed to the growth, insight and learning that comes with each small step that brings them closer to often massive goals.

> *How does one commit to a goal?*

Steven Covey, in *The Seven Habits of Highly Effective People*, states, "One must start with the end in mind." The first step in making any commitment is to envision a desired outcome, goal or target. So take a moment right now to envision your life five years down the road.

In your first scenario, imagine yourself achieving great success. What is your lifestyle? How much income are you generating? Where do you live? How have you changed, grown, become different? What does your business look like? Who are your business partners? How are you known in your community? Now, imagine a scenario where you have not achieved the success your desire, one in which you allow your internal conversation to stop you, things like "It's too hard," "Who do you think you are?" "I am not smart enough," or "I don't have the money." How will your life be different in five years compared to the first scenario? What comes up for you as you compare the two?

What do you do when you imagine? Where are you going? Into the future? Into the realm of possibility? Are you dreaming? The reality is you CREATE! You write a story, your personal movie. We all have the power to create all events as negative or positive, empowering or disempowering. In the first scenario, your creation was one of vision and forward movement. In the second, you envisioned roadblocks and created negative chatter. We create our reality twice: first in our mind, then in our physical reality. The question is, what reality are we willing to commit to? Which story do you want to believe, and which future do you want to embrace? Author and life coach Bill Mayer says, "Where your focus goes, your energy flows." When you commit to something, you make a mental commitment first. Then, through persistence and consistent activity, you manifest your goal, your commitment in the physical.

> *So how do you maintain your*
> *level of commitment?*

Commitment is never complete. It's an ongoing re-creation of a story. When you understand that you are the creator of your own story, you become more conscious of how your thoughts impact your actions. In order to stay committed, it is important to be aware of your thoughts and actions, consciously selecting what is written and what you choose to commit to. When your thoughts and actions are not in alignment with your goals for the future, recommit. I didn't just commit eight years ago to my dream. First I had to commit, then I learned my commitment stays alive by my consciously recommitting to my goals, beliefs and values every day, every hour, and at times moment to moment.

A person who has been a great source of inspiration to me is Jimmy Smith. Living in Pennsylvania, Jimmy is a retired butcher who, at the age of sixty-two, became a professional networker. According to Jimmy, once he understood the numbers related to the business of network marketing, he made a commitment to make an annual income of a million dollars a year. Jimmy states that when he began his journey as a professional network marketer he had much to learn. He experienced neighbors running to the other aisle when they saw him coming in the grocery store, and he also experienced personal bankruptcy. Jimmy enrolled in company after company, studying compensation planes and mastering his craft. He read books, listened to CDs and grew personally, never losing sight of his commitment to earn an annual income of one million dollars. As Jimmy moved from company to company, his income continued to grow; yet he was not close to one million annually. Finally, at the age of seventy-four, Jimmy was introduced to a company called Isagenix International. After studying the compensation plan, the products and the corporation, Jimmy decided to leave an income of over $250,000 per year to pursue his dream. Friends and family thought Jimmy was crazy. Many could not understand why at seventy-four Jimmy would choose to start again. For Jimmy Smith, it was simple. He had committed to a dream and this was his opportunity to fulfill his dream. Within three years of joining Isagenix, Jimmy fulfilled on his personal commitment and earned an annual income of one million dollars. At eighty-five, Jimmy Smith's commitment allows him to earn millions annually and hold the title as the top income earner in Isagenix.

How do you fulfill on a commitment?

We've all seen martial artists breaking boards with their bare hands. The board breaks because you go beyond the board to break it. It's not force that breaks the board, but commitment, focused intention and action. Hitting your target is not enough; you must go beyond your target. Commit to focused intention, look past your target, and keep moving. There will always be moments you want to stop, when you feel like quitting... as soon as you have that negative conversation, remember the definition of commitment. Change the conversation and keep going. In the midst of honoring your commitment, that's when you'll have the conversation with the person that will change the course of your business forever! When you honor your commitments and break through the challenges, success rises up to greet you!

Moving From Good to Great:

1. In what areas of your life and business are you 100% committed?
2. What area can you choose to improve your commitment?
3. What story may you have to rewrite to create a picture that enables you to honor your commitment?
4. What supports or tracking system will you require to honor your commitment?
5. How will honoring your commitment impact your life/business?

2. Urgency:

(Hunger + Initiative) x Time

I am competitive with a desire to be the leader of the pack. I understand that the speed with which I achieve outcomes increases my value.

A leader understands the adage "The speed of the leader is the speed of the pack." They set the pace, the tone and environment that surround their team. Great leaders will always walk with the attitude of getting there first; they tell themselves, "I will not be left behind." They understand that to lead is to always be two steps in front the pack.

Are you leading with a sense of urgency, or are you counting on someone else to set the pace?

Having a sense of urgency can make the difference between thriving as a business and struggling to maintain momentum. A collective sense of urgency can cast a vision that massive results can be created in little time. An image that the energy and time to create small successes can be the same energy that creates massive success. The understanding that it is what you believe you can achieve that determines what you create in a given timeframe. Urgency is a frame of mind, an intention that defines the ease and speed to which a goal is accomplished.

How do you create urgency?

At the core of creating urgency is a firm commitment to the outcome and an unshakable belief in what is possible. As leaders, it's important to create the distinction between realistic goals and having a sense of urgency. They say that there are no unrealistic goals, just unrealistic timeframes. I believe a realistic timeframe is determined by one's sense of urgency. How quickly do you believe you can achieve a goal? What is the cost of not achieving a desired goal, and, most importantly, how hungry are you to achieve a given goal? You see, when one is hungry and filled with desire, urgency is naturally created. When the cost is high, you fill the gap between where you are and where you desire to be with enthusiasm, desire and unshakable belief.

During my time in network marketing, I have noticed it is the individuals who come to a company hungry and with the most to lose have the strongest sense of urgency. It is often those who have lost their source of income or have insufficient income. A great example is a woman by the name of Lynn. When Lynn left her last company to come to her present company, her income went to zero. Having a family to provide for, Lynn's choice was to produce like her family's life depended on it. Lynn came with a sense of urgency many have a hard time understanding. Her attitude was like a warrior who has brought her family to battle and burned her boat in the harbor. Immediate success is the only option or all will perish. Many would say that it was Lynn's past experience that created her results. I believe Lynn's past experience prepared her for this opportunity; however, it was her sense of urgency that allowed her to seize the moment.

What would happen in your business if you set the tone where the only goals worth setting were goals that evoked such passion and enthusiasm within you that urgency was naturally created? What would occur within your business if you became masterful at identifying the cost of not achieving a goal in a specific timeframe? Urgency is created when we perceive we have skin in the game, something on the line. Imagine an organizational culture where urgency and enthusiasm ruled and failure was no longer an option. Like anything else, urgency is a habit. Uncomfortable at first, however, when embraced and cultivated, it becomes the norm. Great leaders are those who are willing to withstand the discomfort and continuously set the pace within their business. They encourage their team members to set lofty goals in what most would believe are unrealistic time frames.

> *Possibility and results become the belief*
> *and mantra within your business.*

Each time someone hits a target, it carves a groove in the subconscious minds of your team members that milestones are possible and easily "do-able." Success becomes the well-worn path that each person walks. What if "possibility and results" become the belief and the mantra within your business? Give your team a roadmap for success. Be an example for others to follow. Put the pedal to the metal, create a sense of urgency and watch magic happen!

Moving From Good to Great:

1. What is one area in your life and business you may need to create a sense of urgency?
2. What is one area in your life/business where you are hungry for change?
3. What is a goal that evokes passion and enthusiasm?
4. What timeframe do you desire to achieve this goal in?
5. What is the cost of not achieving your goal?
6. What impact would achieving your goal have on your life/business?

3. Initiative:

Trust + Intuition + Action

> *I am a focused self-starter; I take action*
> *and trust my intuition.*

Have you ever been to an event where the presenter asks who would like to share or go first? Have you ever encountered that painful moment where the room goes silent and the seconds drag on because no one volunteers to go first? No one risks initiating the conversation or taking action. To have initiative is the simple act of going first, to be the first to share a thought or opinion, ask a question or initiate action.

So why are most of us reluctant to go first and initiate action? I believe it is because for many of us, by the time we were five years old, we were reprimanded for initiating actions and expressing our creativity. We are unconsciously taught that it was bad to fail. As a result, we aspire to be perfect, acting only when we are certain we are able to perform the correct action or give the desired response.

> *My Biggest gift is my willingness to be vulnerable.*
> -Jeff Combs

One of my biggest lessons has been to give up my need to be perfect and risk being transparent and vulnerable. I remember being in a group where we were asked questions. I would sit and rehearse the answer in my mind. My goal was to ensure I said everything just right, or I would wait to see if others answered in a similar manner so I had evidence that my thoughts were valid. However, by the time I had the courage to act, the opportunity to answer the question was gone. The reality is that my opportunity was gone. How many times have you had a brilliant idea? You may have talked about it, thought about it a million times, but never took action. Then one day you are watching TV or a presentation and you see someone getting recognized for your once-original ideas.

> *Initiative is not just for the smartest or richest.*

It is not the smartest or richest people who have built our magnificent communities. Rather, it has been those individuals courageous enough to initiate action. People like you and me who are willing to risk failure to make their idea a reality. Think of Henry Ford and his idea of putting a motor in a car. Everyone thought it was impossible, yet he persisted with his idea. We experience air travel today because of the "crazy" Wright brothers. Think for a moment of the journey of Martin Luther King or Nelson Mandela: both had new ideas for freedom and equality. Both traveled very difficult roads, but their initiative and perseverance has blessed us all.

My best ideas often come in those moments when I have time to relax and daydream. In those moments, when my mind is free, God will gift me with brilliance and I intuitively know I have a great idea. I also know that when I begin to think my new idea through, I will expand that brilliance. However, the more creative the idea, the more likely I am to also experience doubt and fear and begin to question the validity of my gift. The question is will I have the courage to trust my gift and take initiative, or will I give my power over to doubt and fear?

What wonderful idea have you drifted away from?

Napoleon Hill says doubt and fear will cause you to drift away from an original thought in search of approval and social acceptance. Leaders have learned it is their responsibility to be unconventional, trust their intuition and take action on new ideas. Leaders also know that each challenge on their journey to success is not the beginning of failure; rather, it is an opportunity to grow, learn and course-correct. To lead is to go first, initiate action and trust.

How many of you have heard of the company Zappos? Zappos sell shoes on the Internet. When CEO Tony Hsieh came up with the idea to sell shoes online, many believed it would not work. After all, you need to see, feel and try on shoes. Trusting his idea, Hsieh launched a small website selling shoes online. What set Zappos apart and created its success, however, was Hsieh's ingenuity. Not only did he trust his idea to sell shoes online, he trusted new initiatives around customer service and organizational culture that turned out to be genius.

Moving From Good to Great:

1. In what area in your life and business do you show initiative?
2. In what area in your life/business might you require more initiative?
3. What fear might be preventing you from taking action?
4. What impact is your lack of initiative having on your life?
5. What can you do to move past your fear, take action and trust your gifts?
6. How will initiative in this area transform your life/business?

4. Passion:

Desire + Energy

> ***My unwavering belief is
> communicated energetically.***

I believe the source of passion is a strong belief in an idea, or in someone or something. It is a state of mind which creates an energy that can be seen, felt and heard. It is a desire that, when acted upon, can influence and transform people and environments, thus creating change.

Think of when you were a child and you had a desire to get something. It could have been a new bike or something as simple as a candy. As children, we seem programmed to enthusiastically ask for what we want. My mother described me as a little girl who did not understand the word "no." If I wanted something I would ask, ask and ask again. If I heard "no," I might pout or cry. However, once I recovered I would come back with a new reason or perspective and ask again. I would ask until I eventually wore my mother down. You see, my desire and enthusiasm for what I wanted was stronger than my environment.

> *So where does that passion go?*

It is said that the average toddler hears the word "no" 400 times a day. I believe this unconsciously wears us down and conditions us to live small. We show little passion or enthusiasm for what we want, and this shrinks our dreams, goals and desires. We settle for the small things in life, asking only for those things we are certain we will receive. We risk nothing, as we are now conditioned to fear failure, settling for a life that is small and conventional.

Great leaders exhibit a childlike desire.

To effectively lead is to display a childlike desire. It is to have a passion and energy that communicates a level of certainty, a sense of deserving and a relentless determination. Jimmy Smith, a great friend and mentor, is a wonderful example of the mindset of a leader. According to Jimmy, when people say "no" it is because they don't "know" enough. With that mindset and Jimmy's certainty, he will continue to ask, eventually creating the outcome he desires. To have passion is to risk believing that all you desire is possible. It is to move through life with the energy, enthusiasm and the belief of a child.

Moving From Good to Great:

1. Where in your life and business do you exhibit passion?
2. Where in your life/business do you require more passion?
3. What has caused your desire to dwindle or not exist in this area?
4. What can you change to shift your desire and increase your energy in this area?
5. How will an increase in passion impact your results?

She was created for more

Maggie Duffy
Gananoque, Ontario

There was a time in my life where inside of me was a slight whisper that said, "You were created for more." I would feel it, ignore it and delay this feeling often. Why? Well, because I lived in a state of being overwhelmed with complete body inflammation and exhaustion.

I actually thought that since I was in my thirties, this was the way I was supposed to live...tired, overworked and a stressed mom of five.

The good thing is I never did lose my faith while in the depths of despair. I had a prayer that I knew this voice inside needed answered. My prayer was to find a way to be healthy again, to change my financial situation so I could stay at home with my kids, and also to use all my God-given talents and share them completely with the world.

Of course my prayers got answered, bigger and better than I ever thought possible. As my body repaired, so did my mind and my passion for life. I wanted to share with the world everything I was experiencing and I wanted others to benefit completely.

To sit in this place of complete passion, with all your energy flowing into what is possible for everyone you meet, is by far the best feeling in the world. As they say, "Where your focus goes, energy flows."

The habit of passion had completely changed my life, my business and me as a leader. As day-by-day challenges arose I learned to face fear with love and passion. My mission in life was more important than a moment of fear. I would wink at fear and then move on with love and passion to change myself internally each day. I knew the more I grew as a leader the more I could then lead people down a path to greatness for themselves.

Yes, my prayers got answered in a big way and I am forever grateful to God for introducing me to an amazing business and fantastic people to coach and to be coached by. One of these special people in my life is Suzan Hart.

Suzan noticed in me complete passion for what I was doing in the world. I often joked with her that I was like a Tasmanian devil, full of passion and belief, but unless I was harnessed and given direction, I would spin and then not succeed. Thank you Suzan for teaching me to slow down, using steps and systems and yet still allowing me to keep my passion alive with connecting and coaching. I am forever grateful for your leadership, friendship, patience, but mostly for you stopping to see in me a light that was shining brightly with passion. I know you heard my little voice inside me whispering to you, "She was created for more." And you acted on it.

5. Responsibility:

Adapt + Solution Focused + Initiative + Action

> *I respond quickly and adapt easily as
> I face new circumstances.*

Leaders take 100% responsibility for what they create in the world. Your willingness to be responsible is reflected by your ability and willingness to respond and adapt to the circumstances around you. It is the understanding that you have the power to impact all situations by what you say or don't say, or by what you do or don't do. Great leaders understand that to embrace one's power is to take responsibility for all that occurs, positive or negative. It is to avoid casting blame and to learn to respond by asking questions that move you to a solution.

> *How do you take 100% responsibility as a leader?*

One of my biggest lessons over the years has been understanding the personal power that comes with the willingness to be 100% responsible for success and failures. When my business is experiencing massive growth, I am blessed and able to celebrate. When my business is at a standstill, I am responsible for finding a solution. As I built my team, I remember times it became easy to point the finger and blame others for the team's lack of growth. I soon learned that by playing the blame game I gave away my power as I waited for others to effect change. I also learned that my negative energy soon infected my team, and that the faults I saw in each team member were truly a reflection of my own ineffectiveness. I learned that, "as William H. Johnson says, "If it was meant to be, it is up to me." To regain my power and effect change, I had to change. This did not mean I had to do it all; it simply meant I had to take 100% responsibility and be the example of determination and forward movement. It meant I was responsible for what was working and for finding a solution for what was not.

The safest place in the midst of a tornado is in the eye of the storm. The eye of the storm is the place of calm despite the mayhem happening all around. The eye of the storm is a center of peace. The eye of the storm is where energy and direction emerge. To be the eye of the storm is to be grounded and 100% responsible.

In your life and business, you are the eye of the storm. You are the focal point, the place of calm. In order to be the center of calm, as well as the source of energy and direction for your business, you have to take 100% responsibility for it and create a structure around which your business can operate. You have to take 100% responsibility for the mission, culture and results created by your business. This is a simple system I learned from my friend and mentor Bill Walsh. Imagine a box with you in the middle. In the quadrants are: vision, systems, accountability and action. As a leader, you are responsible for creating energy and direction in each of these areas. It is like juggling four balls, keeping each in motion and having the energy rise and fall with precision.

Vision: Your responsibility as a leader is to cast a clear a vision for yourself, your team and business. I have often worked with organizations that have clearly-written missions and visions. These documents sit collecting dust on a shelf or are displayed on a plaque, but are rarely ever read or understood. To effectively cast a vision is to keep it in the forefront of your daily business activities. A vision that lives within a successful business guides all actions and all decisions.

Systems: Have powerful systems in place. This is the track for your business partners to run on. Often, we bring people into our business and they have no idea what to do or where to begin. Ensure that all departments and teams within your business have a turnkey system for all employees, consultants or partners. Having clear systems is the most effective way to have many individuals sending a consistent and clear message. It puts all who participate on the same page while allowing room for individual creativity. Build a system, and constantly evaluate it. Tweak your system when necessary to ensure its effectiveness.

Accountability: My definition of accountability is "being able to account for one's ability." It is to keep a scorecard to monitor the integrity of your plan and evaluate actions while continuously demanding the best and most effective next step. Have successful business implementation markers and systems to track progress and ensure the actions taken are creating the desired results.

Action: The speed of the leader is the speed of the pack. In other words, members of your business will follow the pacing, speed and intensity you model. As you lead, it is your responsibility to set the example. It is your responsibility to be in massive action. If you set the pace, your team members will follow your example. If you are in massive action, chances are your team members will also be in massive action.

Be the eye of the storm

In order to take 100% responsibility for your business you must remain firmly planted in the middle of this box. Many leaders have a tendency to focus on one or two areas and forget the others. A powerful leader knows they are responsible for creating energy in all four areas simultaneously while maintaining balance between them all. An effective leader is eloquent and effective in all four quadrants. A dynamic and productive leader keeps all four balls (quadrants) in the air at once.

One of the best ways to ensure you are the eye of the storm and take 100% responsibility is to be solution focused. To be solution focused is to be grateful for all that comes into your world. It is the attitude that everything is perfect, as all challenges and adversity are an opportunity to grow. It is to ask yourself, "What am I to learn from this situation?" and look to receive the answer. As I learned to be solution focused, I found a new level of internal power.

Moving From Good To Great

1. What areas in your life and business are you taking 100% responsibility?
2. What area might require more of your attention?
3. What might be preventing you from taking 100% responsibility in this area?
4. What solutions can you generate to adapt and create change in this area?
5. What actions can you take to implement your new solutions?
6. How can you create a system that enables others to model the same action?

6. Visionary:

Why + Imagination + Mission + Action

I am a dream builder; I create new realities.

According to the *Encarta* dictionary, a "visionary is somebody of unusually acute foresight and imagination." In my opinion, a true visionary is someone who doesn't only have foresight; it is someone who believes their mission or purpose is to act and create their foresight as a reality. I believe a visionary is someone who has a compelling purpose and mission: a WHY worthy of their life.

When asked, "What is your WHY?" it is to be asked to be the visionary for your life. It is to tap into your imagination and find the fuel that fills your heart and makes you unstoppable. To be a visionary is to look into the future and visualize what you are destined to do and who you are destined to become. To be a visionary is to make your WHY a reality.

What is a WHY?

Your WHY can also be described as a hunger that motivates you to take action. A WHY can be motivated by pain or pleasure. When I took my first step as an entrepreneur, I was motivated by a desire to leave my high-stress job and the constant pain that came with being financially upside down. Although I had many fears, the level of discontent propelled me to act. Today I am motivated by a desire to continuously grow and become more. Although I presently love what I do and I no longer experience financial stress, my motivation comes from a desire to be more, contribute to society, and live my life's purpose. Your WHY is motivated by a desire to be or have more.

> *Ambition flourishes in discontent with the status quo.*
> *Discontent and comfort cannot coexist.*
> -Orrin Woodward

According to Abraham Maslow's hierarchy of needs motivational model, there are five levels of needs. In his model, Maslow suggests that our human needs must be satisfied in a very specific order. We must satisfy each need, beginning with the most basic biological and physical needs, before we can move to the next level. It is only when we satisfy our lower-level needs – which are motivated mainly by deficiencies – that we are able to concentrate on higher-level needs. The motivation that commonly activates your WHY works in a very similar way. We must have our basic needs met before we can effectively cast a vision for a WHY that's primarily focused on contribution and self awareness of our life's purpose

> *Let's explore motivators*

Basic Needs WHY: This is when your WHY is motivated by a basic life need: food, drink, shelter, sleep or bodily well being. They are the basic life necessities we require to comfortably survive. This WHY can be money for food and rent or gas for your car. When establishing your WHY, remember, the mind cannot focus on a higher-level need until your basic needs are taken care of. So if you are challenged financially and there is more month left at the end of your money, focus on the money. Focus on the peace of mind that is available when you become cash-positive and able to fulfill your basic needs with absolute ease.

Material WHY: This is a motivation fueled by all the material things you desire to possess. Simply said, it is the things that money can buy. Your material WHY can be as simple as a new dress and jewels, or as extravagant a multi-million dollar home, a luxury car or a yacht. I have learned that acquisition of material things is often the next natural motivation. The acquisition of material things can be a way to personally affirm our newfound success to ourselves and others. It can also serve to quench the thirst that comes from years of going without.

Recognition WHY: This WHY is also motivated by a desire to be noticed and respected by your family and peers. To be recognized for achievements, contributions, responsibilities, and talents. Although often overlooked by leaders, it has been my experience that many people will do more for recognition than they may do for money. Most people desire to feel valued, respected and honored for what they contribute to the group. Contribution and recognition provide a sense of belonging.

Emotional WHY: This WHY is motivated by a desire for personal growth, fulfillment, self-awareness, as well as purpose. This WHY is often a motivator when the need for money, material things and recognition has been accomplished or satisfied. This motivator is inspired by deeper values and beliefs, or the path we believe we are destined to walk. This WHY may reflect a person's passion, cause or deepest desires. The emotional WHY is often a reflection of how a person would most like to be remembered.

It is said that the journey of a 1000 miles begins with the first step. No matter your circumstances, create a WHY worthy of your life. Remember, what motivates your first WHY may not be the source of motivation for a future WHY. Take your first step. Have unusually acute foresight and become the visionary for your life.

The first visionary I knew personally was my mother Lorna Gordon. Lorna's vision was her family living in North America having access to the resources the world had to offer. Her burning WHY was a desire for her two girls to have an opportunity for a college education and the possibility for a much more abundant life than she had experienced. When Lorna had an opportunity to travel to Canada as part of a dance troupe who performed at Expo 67, she seized the opportunity. With a grade eight education, $20 in her pocket, a lofty vision and a desire for more, Lorna left the Caribbean for Montreal, Canada. Her commitment was to build a life in Canada and return to Trinidad only to get her two girls. Armed with determination, Lorna gained employment as a dancer and within two years she moved her two daughters to Canada. Determined to be an example for her girls, Lorna lived into her vision by finishing high school and getting a college degree. Upon graduation, Lorna went to work in her profession and eventually started her own business. Today Lorna Gordon is retired. Her vision, however, created a clear pathway for her children and grandchildren to follow. Her acute foresight and wiliness to take action will change the lives of generation to come.

Moving From Good to Great:

1. In what areas have you been a visionary and created the outcomes you desired?
2. Where might you be required to use your imagination, cast a vision and develop a WHY worthy of your life?
3. What has stopped you from being the visionary in your life or business?
4. What impact has not continuously expanding your vision had on your life/business?
5. What vision can you cast and what plan can you implement to move you closer to your WHY?
6. How will your new vision and WHY transform your life/business?

7. Solution Focused:

Commitment + Learning + Power

I view each challenge as an opportunity to grow.

What is a barrier or a challenge? I have often heard people describe a challenge as having a hurdle to overcome. Or they will say, "I have hit a wall," "I have a mountain to climb," or "I have the weight of the world on my shoulders." If you use any of these phrases or any that sound like them, I want you to take a moment and examine the energy surrounding these statements. Imagine having to go through life jumping over hurdles. Imagine always having to climb a mountain. Imagine actually walking around with weights on your shoulders as you go through your day. Do you get the picture? These statements all depict situations where your energy is blocked, crushed or you have to over-exert yourself. It is not an image of growth or expansion; rather, it is an image of things almost coming to a grinding halt.

Is your cup half empty, or is your cup half full?

Most of us view a challenge as a big, negative obstacle that will cause pain. We habitually perceive challenges as difficult, stressful and exhausting. We often fear challenge and will do our best to avoid it. We take the "cup half empty" view of a challenge. Now let's shift our energy. Imagine viewing a challenge or barrier as something positive; an event you look forward to, or an opportunity to change and grow. Consider a "cup half full" approach. I have learned that how I deal with any challenge has everything to do with my philosophy, my attitude and focus. I have learned to become solution focused.

Imagine viewing every challenge as an opportunity to bring your business to another level. The reality is that if you have a vision and are living into a WHY worthy of your life, if you have inspiring goals and are following your passion, it makes sense that life would be full of challenges. If I am up to big things, the challenges or barriers will be equally as big. Each challenge I face will be worthy of the magnitude of the life I am designing for myself. Each challenge is the catalyst for growth, expansion and change. Each challenge is designed to mold you into the person who can easily manage the life you are living into.

> *Where your focus goes, your energy flows.*
> -Bill Mayer

This is one of my favorite quotes. It reminds me to focus on what I desire rather than on the challenge or roadblock. It reminds me that, when faced with a challenge, embrace it, view it as an opportunity for learning and a reminder it is time for change. The lesson may be subtle and the required change small. Other times, the change can rock my world and the lesson can change the direction of my life. Where your focus goes is truly key. When you focus on the problem, you give the problem energy and it expands. Have you ever had something go wrong and you choose to whine and complain about it? You take on suffering and you engage all your friends in the "poor me" discussion. It soon becomes what everyone is talking about. The problem expands as the focus consumes your time and energy, yet you are not moving forward.

When you focus on the solution, you keep your mind's eye focused on what you want, or where you are going. Being solution focused instantly gets your energy moving forward. It is like using a flashlight to guide you out of a dark place. Although you hold the flashlight, you focus on the light as it guides you forward. By focusing on what you want, your mind instantly begins to search for answers, and in doing so you begin to ask solution-focused questions, powerful questions designed to pull you forward, moving you closer to a solution.

Steps to Becoming Solution Focused

1. Recognize when you are stopped: Common feelings are fear, nervousness, frustration, anger or intense discomfort. The first step is to acknowledge your feelings.

2. Choose how you are going to manage your feelings: You can choose to suffer and create "trauma and drama" in your life. You can also choose to acknowledge the feelings and work towards a solution. Remember: suffering is optional.

3. Share your feelings and thoughts with a friend or mentor: Our challenges are often caused by conscious or unconscious issues from our past, or incidents and negative experiences we carry into our present. Your goal is to begin to understand the source of the feeling and work through it. Remember, no feeling or thought is ridiculous during this process. This is your search for understanding. Understanding will allow you to create a clearing for new behaviors and begin moving towards a solution.

4. Ask yourself "What am I to learn from this situation?" When you embrace the challenge, you will no longer expend energy by resisting or fighting. You will see the hurdles, the mountain and the weight on your shoulders as self-imposed. You will notice that the stress you are experiencing is your own resistance to change. Imagine being in a lake and swimming against the current. Imagine attempting to walk into a wind. Now imagine ease. To embrace the challenge is to embrace change and allow life to reveal the lesson to you.

5. Sit with the learning: Breathe out the fear. Trust your intuition and remain open.

6. Focus on the solution: Remember: Where your focus goes, your energy flows. If you focus on the solution, you will begin to create positive, forward-moving thoughts. Begin by visualizing the result you desire. By doing this, you will begin to attract what you require and become aware of new circumstances that once had no significance. In your quest for a solution, you will become attracted to books, tapes, events and people who will help you move forward. You will begin to ask powerful, forward-moving questions. Finally, you will begin to see your challenge as a gift, one that opens a whole new world of possibilities.

7. Create behaviors that facilitate change: Internal understanding of any issue only becomes reality when attached to clear and specific action. Adopt new behaviors that will move you towards your goal. Create new habits.

8. Act in spite of fear or discomfort: New behaviors only become habits with intensity and persistent, consistent action.

Moving From Good to Great:

1. In what areas in your life and business have you been solution focused?
2. Where might you be required to be solution focused?
3. What fears, behaviors, attitudes or challenges may be stopping you from becoming solution focused?
4. How is your present behavior and attitude impacting your life/business?
5. What steps can you choose to take to create a solution?
6. What might you learn in the process of being solution focused?
7. How will this new focus on solutions impact your life/business?

Ready for the next challenge

Shannon O'Neil
Sydenham, Ontario

Not that long ago when I would find myself faced with a problem, as we often do in life, I would spend a significant amount of time analyzing, wondering why the problem had occurred, what I should have done to avoid the problem, how the problem happened and, depending on the situation, who had contributed to the problem. Although I believed that spending a lot of time focusing on the problem and all factors surrounding it was beneficial to preventing it from re-occurring, it would happen that the same problem would constantly re-appear in my life. What I did not realize at the time was that I was *Problem Focused*.

What I was actually doing was recreating my problem over and over again. By focusing on the logistics of the problem itself, I was putting all my energy into managing and evaluating. Doesn't sound like too much fun, does it? Evidence showed that it was not very productive either.

About three years ago I had the amazing opportunity to begin a career of working from home allowing me to be a full-time mother to my beautiful daughter Ava. You can only imagine the list of new problems I faced switching my schedule and mindset from employee to entrepreneur, and from wife to mother (not to mention maid, chauffeur, chef, nurse, etc.) My only saving grace was that I was blessed to have taken the entrepreneurial position working intimately with Suzan Hart.

It did not take me long to realize that Suzan worked in a way that I had not seen while working as an employee. What I called "problems," Suzan called 'challenges." When I would ask *Why*, Suzan would gently remind me that in most instances *Why* is irrelevant. When I would talk about the "problem," Suzan would guide me towards discussing possible solutions. While I had only known and witnessed how to be *Problem Focused*, Suzan introduced me to the incredible habit of being *Solution Focused*.

I now take on the habit of being Solution Focused every day. I no longer have problems showing up in my life; instead I have challenges that are just waiting for a solution. The wonderful thing about challenges is that once you solve them...they disappear! Once you solve a challenge, you gain confidence in your ability to solve the next. Being solution focused is not just beneficial in my professional tasks and relationships; it spills over to every area of my life and makes me a better mother, wife and friend.

I have learned that when you are Solution Focused vs. Problem Focused, the solutions to your challenges come quicker, clearer and with more conviction than what was ever possible before. Challenges do not slow you down; instead, they excite and motivate you, they induce creativity, brainstorming and insightful discussion.

Embodying the habit of being Solution Focused has touched every area of my life. I find myself empowered, inspired and ready for the next challenge.

8. Courage:

Open Mind + Discernment + Risk + Action

> *I take risks and act in spite of my fears.*
> *I am willing to step into the unknown and*
> *expand my comfort zone.*

According to *Webster's Dictionary*, to have courage is to have "the quality of mind which enables men to encounter danger or difficulty with firmness or without fear or depression or spirit." It is the willingness to risk, to act in the face of fear and expand one's comfort zone. It is to feel the fear, be discerning and take action. Interestingly, "to risk" is defined as being willing to do something that involves the possibility of injury, damage or loss. In my opinion, to be a risk taker is to be willing to have the courage to evaluate the potential risk and take calculated actions with the belief of an expected positive outcome. Having the courage to take a risk is the determining factor that can separate those who create success from those who do not.

> *Do you have the courage to risk*
> *failing to create success?*

I remember when I first decided to take my first step as a full-time network marketer. Most people thought I was crazy. I heard things like "Those types of businesses rarely ever succeed" and "Why would you give up the security of a full time job?" What I was really hearing was the fear being expressed by my friends and family. They were not willing to risk without the guarantee of success. As I listened and felt the tension around me, I had to ask myself some important questions: What is security and what does it mean to risk? Do I have the courage to risk failing to create the success I desire?

What is security and what does it mean to risk?

Let's look at the word "security." *Webster's Dictionary* defines security as "a feeling of confidence and safety" or "a predictable routine or situation." For many people, having security is being able to know the outcome before they begin the journey. I go to work and at the end of the week I am guaranteed a paycheque for the hours I have worked. The question is whether or not that really is security.

Through my own experiences, I have come to learn that security can only truly occur when I am the one in charge of deciding my own destiny. I remember the day I walked into work and found my belongings packed up in a box. I was not being fired for anything I had done wrong. Their reasoning was that I had produced too efficiently, and somehow that was a problem. It was in that moment that I realized I was not secure because someone else was controlling my job and ultimately my paycheque.

I also remember when I was not making enough money to provide for my family. Although I was guaranteed an income, it was just not enough. I believed I deserved more, but access to more income was not in my control. All I had to show for my hard work was worry and stress. I felt anything but secure. As it turned out, leaving my life in the hands of others had proven to be a risk in itself, leaving me with little or no influence over my own destiny. The real question was, did I have the courage to trust my ability and be paid for the result I created? Was I willing to face my fear and courageously step outside my comfort zone?

If my illusion of security had proven to be risky, what does it mean to risk? Going back to its dictionary definition, to risk is to be willing to do something that involves the possibility of injury, damage or loss. However, is there truly anything we do in life that does not have a degree of possibility of injury, damage or loss? The real question is what the degree of risk is, and what can be done to reduce the possibility of that potential risk.

> *What can be done to reduce potential risk?*

Successful leaders are courageous. They understand that risk is part of living a bold and magnificent life. The answer is not to eliminate risk, but instead to understand the potential risk, and then plan accordingly. I believe that most people fear risk because they fail to set specific and measureable goals, consequently failing to implement a strategic plan to achieve their goals.

As I was planning to leave my job and become fully self employed, the world around me was panicked and up in arms about my decision. I, however, remained calm. I remained calm because I had a plan. I had looked at a number of scenarios, both good and bad, putting in place a plan to address each potential circumstance. My plan for leaving my job had begun more than a year prior to the date of execution. Once I created my plan, I focused on nothing but success. My plan gave me a feeling of security and that left me feeling that I had prepared for the potential risk.

After being self-employed for over five years, I understand that although there are no guarantees, I feel secure in my ability to make decisions that impact my destiny. I realize I create my own security by being willing to take 100% responsibility for the forward movement of my own life. I now know that the only devastating risk is to lack courage and never risk at all. I've learned from my hardships, and having the courage to embrace new adventures allowed me to give myself new opportunities. It has built the muscles that keep me focused on the solution. Taking a risk and succeeding creates the confidence and internal power that makes leaders magnetic.

> *Act in spite of your fears.*

I once had the privilege of spending three days with a group of dynamic entrepreneurs. The diversity in the group made for stimulating conversations and a fertile learning environment. During our three days, we were exposed to a series of activities that challenged us physically, emotionally and spiritually. As we engaged in these activities, I witnessed transformations both big and small. Each individual demonstrated a level of courage I knew they would be able to draw on as they returned to their boardrooms, conference calls and presentations.

One woman's willingness to grow inspired me, and provided me with a valuable lesson. As the facilitator gave us our instructions, I could sense her anxiety was higher than that of the other participants. I noticed she had a difficult time concentrating. I was aware that she was allowing her mind to race forward, creating horrifying scenarios in her imagination. She was gripped with fear. On several occasions she had to be reminded to breathe. In reality, the activities had not even begun. We were simply sitting in chairs, listening to instructions.

Luckily, this woman was open to coaching and was willing to be supported by the group. In spite of her anxiety, she pressed on and completed each exercise. The stress of the day left her exhausted, yet empowered. She was moved that she had the courage to face her fear and acted anyway. I asked her what she had received from completing the exercises, and she said, "Suffering is optional." She explained that by imagining horrifying scenarios, she was creating and choosing her own suffering. She now had the awareness that she had choices. She could choose to be grounded in the present, or run into the future, imagining the worst. She recalled the times she had allowed herself to be stopped by her own chaos, fear and drama. She became aware of the opportunities she had missed by creating stress and drama in her mind. She realized how she had limited her life by allowing her fear to limit her choices.

How often have you allowed your mind to take you out of the present by imagining the worst? How often have you allowed your imagination and fear to stop you from an experience that could change your life? I have had the opportunity to speak with this woman on several occasions since the event. I am struck by how much she has changed. I am inspired by her courage and her willingness to choose opportunity in spite of her fear.

As I reflect on my life, I can see the times I chose to suffer and missed an opportunity to experience possibility. Suffering has many faces. Mental suffering, especially at your own hands, can be just as debilitating as physical suffering. I invite you to choose to be courageous. Be mindful and conscious of your choices. In the words of my dear friend, remember: "Suffering is optional."

Moving From Good to Great:

1. Where in your life and business have you been courageous?
2. What area in your life/business might additional courage be required?
3. What is the fear that has you stopped?
4. What is the impact of this fear on your life/business?
5. What can you do to take your first courageous step?
6. How will this first step impact your life/business?

Pick yourself up and keep moving

Fozia Murtaza
Whitby, Ontario

> *"I learned that courage was not the absence of fear,*
> *but the triumph over it. The brave man is not he who*
> *does not feel afraid, but he who conquers that fear."*
> - Nelson Mandela

It would take me years to understand the meaning of these powerful words. My whole life, I have admired those with courage. How I desired to be like them. Fearless, no matter what hurdle they faced, they kept going. I could only dream of being like that. My reality was quite the opposite. Married at only eighteen, I went from my parents taking care of me to my husband taking care of me. The next twenty-something years went by so quick and the next thing I knew, my kids were in their twenties. Although I had managed to go to college, and I had worked over the years, I never pursued a career because I was taken care of. I had this life that seemed perfect to others. But something was missing. I was grateful for all my blessings, but I was not happy with who I had become. I felt disconnected with myself. I had to change that...but how? I needed to become independent...but where to begin? I started my personal development journey. This was about mind, body, and spirit. I needed a makeover!

It's funny how when you are ready for something, that is when it shows up in your life. I was introduced to Suzan Hart. Suzan inspired me. She became my coach, my mentor, and my friend. The following years, I made many changes and learned that I could take care of myself.

I was so proud of myself. Excess weight started to come off. I had a fabulous support group. I was helping others to transform their lives. I was making a difference. Then it happened. My husband suffered a heart attack. Thank God he was going to be alright. However, he was unable to return to work or take care of any of the other things that he had always taken care of. Everything changed. Aside from taking care of him and being the strong one for the kids, for the first time in my life I was faced with handling the income and paying the bills. I had worked so hard to be strong and courageous enough to change my life, but now I was paralyzed. I told myself this was too much to deal with. Old habits started to creep back in. I wanted to run away. I avoided phone calls from my support group. I stopped eating healthily. I felt my journey had come to an end.

It was a conversation with Suzan that made me realize the meaning of the powerful words of Nelson Mandela. Everything I had accomplished had prepared me for this moment. Being courageous was not about being fearless. It was not about having the answers or solution to deal with the situation. Being courageous was about moving forward despite my feeling of being paralyzed. Courage was being able to give attention to the situation. Courage was that I didn't run away. It was during that conversation that I realized that courage is to be committed enough to pick yourself up and keep moving regardless of how many times you may fall.

9. Guiding Principles:

Values + Awareness + Commitment + Integrity

> *My actions and decisions are in alignment with my values. I am conscious of the principles that guide my actions.*

Many cars nowadays have a GPS. My previous car had On Star: I'd hit a button, and a nice lady or guy would greet me and offer to help me navigate to my destination. They would punch in the coordinates, and I'd get directions to my desired location. I have my own personal GPS to navigate my life. I call it my GPS, my Guiding Principles for Success. I have eight principles or values that, like the correct coordinates to a destination, guide my choices and impact my behaviors and decisions. My Guiding Principles of Success are posted on the wall in my office. I carry them written in my wallet. I know them by heart. I live my life and make my decisions by my personal GPS. When I am stressed, overwhelmed or uncertain, I can always track the challenge back to my thoughts and actions being out of alignment with one or two of my Guiding Principles for Success.

> *What are your Guiding Principles for Success?*

To utilize your personal GPS, you must be clear on what values guide you. What values are important to you?

What values enable you to continuously recreate a sense of peace and alignment in your life? Once you're clear on your Guiding Principles, decisions come easily and success is a given. Having a GPS is important in leading self, and integral to leading others. Your personal GPS sets the stage for how you'll operate, who you become in the world, and how you will be known.

Are You Using Your GPS?

How many times have you seen a leader make a decision that is biased, based on whether or not they liked someone, or from anger or stress? Hold onto this vision through the lens of leadership: When a leader makes decisions not grounded in guiding principles or values, it says to people, "I am inconsistent, I make decisions based on my likes and dislikes, if it's easy or hard, whether I'm tired or rested. In other words, I make decisions based on what serves me."

This is human nature. We tend to gravitate to decisions that sit within our comfort zone. However, when you make decisions against the backdrop of your Guiding Principles, you don't make the easy decision; you make the best decision. When you make decisions based on your Guiding Principles, it is an indicator that your leadership is consistent, that you are fair and that you believe in equity. Equity does not mean you treat everyone the same. Equity means that you use your GPS to make decisions. Knowing an individual's circumstances may dictate a different decision for them than for someone else. The only way you can make an equitable and fair decision (not the same decision) is if you are guided by something that's larger than you.

Are you guided by values that are larger than you?

I believe that our Guiding Principles for Success are divinely inspired; they come from a bigger place. These principles cause us to rise to the occasion and operate from a higher place and be better people. Your GPS is most beneficial when you're angry and you want to lash out emotionally. When guided by your GPS, you are able to detach from a situation, and respond rather than react. Your GPS allows you to create recovery; you leave people with a feeling of being whole and complete. Guided by your GPS, you evaluate behaviors rather than attack the person.

Great leaders know their GPS is the anchor and the foundation of their leadership. Leaders who operate from a GPS create positive team cultures and environments of clarity and consistency. Difficult decisions are more often accepted because team members trust that decisions are made against the backdrop of a solid GPS. By making your guiding principles clear, they eventually become the principles that guide the team. A clear GPS ultimately creates an environment where accountability is expected and equitable treatment becomes the norm.

Moving From Good to Great:

1. What are your existing guiding principles for success?
2. How effectively are you at using your GPS to make decisions and guide your actions?
3. What is the impact when you effectively use your GPS?
4. What is the impact when you have not used your GPS?
5. What decisions or actions might you have to re-evaluate using your GPS?
6. How will re-evaluating this decision impact your life/business?

10. Objective:

Open + Discernment + Choice

> *I respond rather than react to the events that occur around me.*

To be objective is one of the most powerful skills a leader can posses. To be objective is to be unbiased and open to all possibilities. *Webster's Dictionary* defines "objective" as what is formed by the mind. In other words, what is created by what Landmark Education calls the "meaning-making machine," the mind. To be objective is to learn the distinction between attachment and commitment.

Have you ever been in a situation where something occurred, you reacted, and you jumped to a conclusion? In that moment you painted a picture and created a story that you related to as a fact, the absolute truth, or the real deal. We become emotionally attached to our story, allowing our perception of the event to determine how we feel. We let an external circumstance determine if we are on a high, full of excitement and enthusiasm, or if we are experiencing a low, filled with fear, despair and doubt. You see, when something in our world occurs, we write our own unique story; then we relate to that story as the only truth. We become attached.

> *Are you attached or committed?*

To be objective is to be unattached to the story. It is the

ability to see your perspective or point of view while being able to see another's perspective or story. When circumstances occur, great leaders are able to look from an unattached place to the various vantage points. The question is, how do you remain unattached to your own story? The answer is to be committed.

When I am committed, I do my best to move towards a goal with laser focus. However, as events occur, I am able to step back, manage my emotions and look at a situation as if I were a neutral observer. At times, the new information I am able to obtain from my neutral space may have me change course, adjust my action, or even provide me with a new perspective while I move towards my target. To be objective is to allow data to come in from the world, assess it, and use the information. To be objective is to surrender. It is to have faith and trust the process called life.

When I did family counseling, I had a young boy named Gary on my caseload. Most would describe Gary as disruptive in the classroom. For years, teachers complained about his inability to concentrate, and as a result, this young boy spent many of his days in detention or at the office. Most teachers knew of Gary and his siblings' history and seemed to dread having him assigned to their classes. As he entered grade four, he was assigned to the classroom of a young male teacher. This young teacher was energetic and used many interactive exercises in his classroom. More importantly, this young new teacher knew little of Gary's history and was committed to having all his students succeed. That year, Gary excelled and spent no time in detention. The new male teacher saw Gary as above average in intelligence and described him as being bored with the regular curriculum. As a result of the open mind of the new young teacher, Gary excelled in school that year and went on to have a successful academic experience.

Steps to remain objective

1. **Determine the facts:** What actually occurred. This is the event. Something you can observe or measure. The fact is void of your interpretation. *"Bob is sitting on the stoop outside the house."*
2. **Determine opinions:** These are the possible interpretations of the facts, a person's perception of the event. *"Bob is locked out of the house."* Or *"Bob is enjoying the beautiful evening."*
3. **Determine the predominant beliefs:** Common conditioned thoughts or expected outcomes about an event. *"Bob always forgets his keys."* *"Bob likes to watch the stars."*

As you can see from the example above, our beliefs often color our perception of an event, which in turn creates the story we move forward with. To be objective is one's ability to distinguish between the event that occurred and all the stuff we bring to the table. It is to separate out our story and our beliefs from the actual event. It is only when we are committed to understanding the facts that we are able suspend judgment, be objective and respond rather than react.

Moving From Good to Great:

1. Where have you made objective decisions or judgments in your life and business?
2. Where might you be attached to your point of view?
3. How might your lack of objectiveness impact your life/business?
4. What can you do to become more objective in this area?
5. How will your commitment to being objective impact your life/business?

11. Integrity:

(Honesty + Guiding Principles) x Time

I honor my word. I am reliable. I follow through.

Have you ever experienced being told what to do? How did that feel? Did you feel defiant, resentful or disempowered? When someone is told what to do, resistance and negative emotions arise. However, when a leader sets the example, they ETR. They "earn the right" to ask others to take action. To earn the right is to have your leadership sit on a foundation of integrity. When ETR occurs, team members are influenced. They take action from a place of inspiration rather than resentment and coercion.

Have You Earned the Right?

Leadership based on integrity begins by setting the example of bold action. To be an effective leader is to be in action. Most people have a tendency to manage rather than lead. To manage is rather passive. It is to instruct, tell and demand. To lead with integrity is to be active. It is to model, be the example and set the pace. To lead from a place of integrity does not mean I must do everything myself. It is to lead from a foundational philosophy of "I am not willing ask others to do something I am not willing to do myself." It is to own that which you teach or ask of others. It is to understand that people are not inspired by perfection. Rather, they are inspired by the humanity of being willing to serve and contribute. Or risk being vulnerable and moving from good to great in an area they may have previously been uncomfortable. It is to understand that inspiration causes action.

> *As I grow older, I pay less attention to what people say. I just watch what they do.*
> -Andrew Carnegie

Integrity is fluid and is re-created moment to moment. According to the dictionary, integrity is "the quality of possessing and steadfastly adhering to high moral principles or professional standards." Landmark Education simply says integrity is to "be your word." To do what you say you are going to do when you say you are going to do it. To have integrity is to make right a wrong and own your mistakes. It is to follow through on commitments, and when you fall short, to re-commit.

> *How do you maintain integrity?*

To create integrity is to understand that our mind spends most of it time out of integrity and, if unchecked, we will create behaviors that are out of integrity. To check your mind is to know integrity is a process of committing – and re-committing – to actions that have you be your word. I might commit to work out every morning. My alarm goes off and my mind says, "You are too tired, sleep for another hour." To check my mind is to say, "I committed to working out and I choose to honor my word." The action is then jumping out of bed and going to work out rather than curling up in bed for another hour. I re-commit and be my word.

Moving From Good to Great:

1. In what area in your life and business do you have a high level of integrity?
2. Where might it be required to improve your level of integrity?
3. What impact does your lack of integrity in this area have on your life/business?
4. What plan can you put in place to re-create integrity in this area?
5. How will re-creating integrity in this area impact your life/business?

Who is your daughter most like?

Cindy Salter
Montreal, Quebec

I have learned that integrity is to lead by example doing the thing you said you would do: "walking the talk." This lesson could not be more apparent than in my journey raising my two beautiful daughters, Devon and Darrion.

Although I would give my daughters what I believed to be good advice, I would at times notice a reluctance to act. It was as if they resisted my council due to a lack of confidence or fear. I knew they had all the gifts necessary to succeed; the question was why, they at times, resisted taking action.

I remember sharing my concern about one of my daughters with Suzan. She listened then asked me a simple yet powerful question, "Who is your daughter most like?" As I paused, a level of insight emerged that would change my future. I realized that my daughters were modeling the example I was setting. I would say one thing, yet I would do another. I would often avoid new experiences because I lacked confidence or was fearful. I was setting the example that the unknown was scary.

In an effort to recreate integrity, I had an open and honest discussion with my daughters. I acknowledged that I had at times not set the best example. I let them know that my behavior would change and I would be the example rather than provide lip service.

As I have worked to change my behavior I have watched my daughters also change. They are taking risks and trying new things. The habit of integrity is to truly be the example and trust that you will inspire change through your actions.

12. Persistence:

(Passion + Practice + Patience) x Time

> *I am patient. I take consistent productive*
> *action until I accomplish my goal.*

When I was eleven years old, my mother sent me to a summer camp called Parkside Ranch. I believe her goal was to keep an overly active tomboy occupied and out of trouble. At this camp, I created some of my best childhood memories and learned lessons I carry with me today. We learned to ride horses, pitch a tent, kayak, fire a rifle, and master archery. Although I loved each activity, my absolute favorite was archery. At the archery range, I learned a valuable lesson I still use today.

> *Do you have passion?*

I remember my first day at the archery range. I was excited and nervous. The thought of firing a bow and arrow seemed so adult. I could not wait to have my first arrow sail through the air and pierce the target. I could not wait to hit the bull's-eye. When my turn came, my instructor showed me how to stand. He gave me specific instructions on how to hold the bow. I remember him telling me to hook the arrow in the string and gently lay it along the rib on the bow. He then instructed me to slowly pull the string back and release the arrow. I followed each and every instruction. I can still remember the sharp pain of the string hitting my forearm and the arrow falling about two feet in front of me. Excited and determined to have success, I continued shooting arrow after arrow with no success. That day, as I left the range, my instructor congratulated me for my passion and enthusiasm. He told me that a big part of success was having a passion for what one was doing.

> *Are you willing to practice?*

The next day I returned to the range armed with my passion for my newfound sport. Once again, I shot arrow after arrow and very little changed. Now I was frustrated: Why could I not get the stupid arrow to sail through the air? I remember thinking, "Forget passion! I am done." At that moment, my instructor again intervened. He said, "Suzan, you have to be persistent. To release an arrow so that it hits your target demands a series of well-executed movements. It may appear that I (the coach) am just picking up the arrow and pulling the string, but I have learned very specific skills. You have to give yourself enough time to learn the skills and techniques to be successful."

For the next few weeks I focused on my technique. I practiced how to hold the bow, how to position my arm. I focused on how to have the string roll off my finger, and the precise time to release the arrow. I began to go to the range twice a day. I was determined to master my new skills. My arrow had begun to fly through the air, but it was not going anywhere close to the target. Again I became frustrated. Again I was ready to quit.

> *Will you exercise patience?*

This time my instructor had a new lesson for me. He told me that he was impressed with my passion and willingness to practice. However, I now had to learn patience. He told me that most people quit just before they hit the target. He encouraged me to keep coming to the range. He shared with me that I had learned new skills, but they had not yet become a part of me. He encouraged me to go to the range, focus on my target, and begin to feel the movement rather that think about the movement. He insisted that if I were patient, I would soon hit my target.

Trusting the words of my instructor, I continued to return to the range twice a day. I remember staring at the target and allowing myself to feel the motions. Each time I pulled the string back, I instinctively could feel when to release, and each time I got closer to my target. Within a few days, I hit the outer ring of the target. A few days later I hit the second ring on the target. Then came THE day! I remember staring at the bulls-eye, lifting the bow and pulling back the string. As I released the string and the arrow cut through the air, I heard a whooshing sound and then a "thud." I had hit the bull's-eye!

Do you own your space?

To be persistent is to pursue a worthy objective until it is complete. To do so, one must be willing to expand, grow, overcome challenges and face setbacks. I have learned that it is the level of motivation or passion that has often inspired me to act. However, it is my willingness to withstand discomfort, practice new skills, and learn new lessons that most often moves me towards my goal. It is to have the patience to put in my

10,000 hours that created the space for persistence to be born, allowing me to master my new skill and eventually take my place and powerfully own my space.

Moving From Good to Great:

1. What are the areas in your life and business where you presently reap the rewards of persistence?
2. In what area might you be required to be more persistent?
3. What is the impact of your lack of persistence in your life/business?
4. What plan can you put in place to ensure your persistence?
5. Who could you connect with to ensure you are accountable?
6. How will your persistence in this area impact your life/business?

13. Contribution:

Gratitude + Vision + Initiative

> **I give consistently to my community:**
> **time, money, and service.**

To contribute is to give. I have learned that true contribution occurs when I am able to freely give and have no expectations. It is to give from a place of total gratitude and the belief in abundance of our world. It is to know that I am always able to give and make a valuable contribution to the world around me. I have often heard people say, "I have nothing to give. I barely have two pennies to rub together." I believe that it is in the times when I have struggled that contribution has served me most. I remember when I was financially upside down and life felt like an uphill climb. In my darkest times, it seemed like nothing was going right. Life felt like a struggle and I was consumed with worry, frustration and fear. It was easy to focus on what was not working in my life, play the victim and be consumed with self-pity.

> *I have learned to give of my time.*

Luckily for me, when my life was the most upside down, I was also blessed to be the manager of one of the largest drop-in centres in the city of Toronto. One of the groups we provided service for was women who were homeless. On a daily basis, we provided shelter from

Mother Nature, showers and clean clothing, as well as a warm meal and friendly conversation or guidance. Over the years I worked at the drop-in, it rarely was a nine-to-five job; rather, it was a service. To serve meant to contribute what was needed when it was needed. To serve was to suspend judgment, step into understanding and find a solution. Over the years, I was continually amazed at the strength of the human spirit. Each day I would watch women who had spent the night sleeping outside enter the drop-in and be consumed with gratitude for a warm meal and quiet place to sit. Being able to give served to remind me that my life was truly abundant. It reminded me to be grateful for all the blessings I did have and gave me the strength and the courage to continue on. Today when life throws me a curve, I have learned to embrace it and welcome the lesson. I have also learned that it is also the best time to contribute, as it serves to remind me I have yet to experience a truly bad day.

> *I have learned to tithe 5% of my income.*

It was also during my most difficult time financially that I learned the power of contribution. I remember sitting in at a T. Harv Eker "Millionaire Mind Intensive," and the trainer, David Wood, encouraging the audience to donate 5% of their income. Of course my mind began to scream, "I have no money! I have nothing to contribute!" The words he spoke next have continued to guide me. David said, "It's not the amount; it is the habit." It actually is the ability to sit in gratitude for what you have, to expect more is on its way, and consciously choose to contribute.

Most people believe they must wait until they have

extra before they contribute any money. Unfortunately, the extra never comes. What we want expands faster than what we have. Great leaders understand the power of contribution. You see, it is the habit of contribution that actually creates the space for more money. After attending the MMI, I decided to trust and sit in the belief that my life was abundant and great things were on their way. I immediately began to contribute a portion of my earnings. At first it truly was just pennies. However, the more I contributed, the more blessed I began to feel and the more I began to receive. As I contributed, I watched my income grow to levels I had once only dreamed of. Through the act of contribution, I began to experience abundance and I began to expect more.

I have learned to give of my mind and spirit.

To contribute is not only about money and time; it is also to initiate action, share new ideas, and bless the world with your unique brilliance and creativity. To contribute is to be willing to risk putting yourself out in the world. Think of all the advantages we have today because someone had an idea they were willing to trust and create as reality. Today we can fly because of the contributions of the Wright brothers. We now communicate with devices that fit in the palm of our hand because of men like Steve Jobs who had the courage to push the envelope and continuously dream bigger. I know I have the courage to share my brilliance because of women like Oprah, who was willing to have a voice and share her ideas.

What new idea will you contribute? How will you use your creativity to bless the world? What organization will you give your time to? What percentage of your income will you tithe? To contribute is to believe in the abundance of your life. It is to keep the energy that comes to you in flow by passing it on and blessing others. It is to know that we are both the blessed and the blessing.

Bonus 2: At www.hartzone.com, we have many gifted writers who regularly contribute to the HartZone readers. Register for our mailing list and receive weekly articles from our contributing authors.

Moving From Good to Great:

1. How have you contributed to others in your community?
2. What has been the impact of your contribution on your business/life and those of others?
3. What might be an area in which you have been reluctant to contribute?
4. How could you contribute in this area?
5. What will be the impact of your contribution on your business/life and those of others?

14. Influence:

(Self Mastery + Responsibility + Values + Action) x Time

I inspire others to take action.

According to John C. Maxwell, leadership is "the ability to obtain followers." Fred Smith says, "Leadership is getting people to work for you when they are not obligated." In other words, your level of leadership is determined by your ability to influence others. I define influence as "one's ability to inspire others to take action."

So what creates influence?

I believe that my influence is directly related to my level of self-mastery. You see, the first person I must lead or influence is the person I see when I look in the mirror. Often, this is the most difficult person to lead. My leadership is determined by my willingness to be 100% responsible for what I create in the world. Influence is created through who I am and how I consistently show up in the world. My ability to lead is silently judged by whether I am willing to take a risk when fearful or uncertain. Will I be punctual or follow through on a commitment when I am tired or exhausted? Do I exhibit initiative when others are not willing to act? Am I solution focused when confronted with a problem? Do I have vision when there appears to be nothing ahead?

Am I guided by integrity and clear values when tempted by an easy or less ethical solution? Most importantly, my leadership and influence is determined by how I treat a stranger when I believe no one is looking.

> *What principles, thoughts and*
> *values guide your actions?*

I have learned that my level of influence is determined by the principles, thoughts and values that guide my actions. My leadership is a direct measurement of my internal strength, attitude and belief systems. I have also learned that the action or behavior that inspires one person may have little impact on another. Therefore, the more areas in which I develop mastery, the broader my influence. I have met many individuals who are inspired by my organizational skills and my ability to create systems. As a result, they are inspired to model that behavior. Other individuals are inspired by my willingness to be transparent and to risk being vulnerable. You see, each of us is attracted to and will follow that which inspires us.

> *Be the first person you are willing to lead,*
> *and inspire others to follow.*

Great leaders know influence is not created through coercion or fear, or from the power that comes with a title or position. Think for a moment of the people who have had the most influence in your life. These often are parents, teachers, coaches and mentors whose habits and behaviors shaped who you are today. Some behaviors you may have consciously modeled, and others may have unknowingly become part of your way of being. Most often, it was not what they told you to do that had the most influence; it was who they were willing to be and what they modeled that shaped who you have become. I remember my basketball coach, Mr. Don Caldwell. I would describe him as a man of few words, yet he was a profound role model for many young athletes. As an impressionable teen, I was impressed with the level of consistency and discipline he modeled. He was always punctual, prepared and organized. He demonstrated an impressive work ethic and was a master at his craft. He expected nothing but the best from himself and all the athletes he coached. Mr. Caldwell shaped the lives of many young athletes and influenced the men and women they have become.

Influence occurs when what you say is consistently in alignment with what you do. It is created when people can count on who you are and how you show up. Influence is the compounded effect of positive or negative habits over time. It can work to move you towards a goal or move you away from a goal. Influence will consistently shape the character and reputation you are known for.

Moving From Good to Great:

1. Where in your business or life do you have influence?
2. What has been the impact of that influence?
3. Where might you have a desire to improve or shift the influence you have?
4. What will you have to change or improve in order to create the level of influence you desire?
5. What impact will this new level of influence have on your business/life?

15. Power:

(Discernment + Integrity + Influence + Experience) x Time

> *I have inner confidence. I posses an emotional maturity that results from my growth and experience. I affect and influence my environment.*

I have worked with and managed teams for over twenty years. One topic that continues to fascinate me is power. The power dynamic that exists between team members and how a leader's perception of power can either create a positive, healthy environment or one that is abusive, competitive and unhealthy. I soon learned that to be an effective leader, one had to be comfortable with the level of power that comes with their leadership position and, most importantly, understand the dynamics related to power.

> *Do you have power? Are you comfortable with power?*

Whenever I arrived at a new location, one of the first trainings would focus on power dynamics. To begin the training, I would ask the staff, "Who in the room believes they have power?" It always fascinated me that no one in the room would raise their hand. I would follow my question with the statement, "I believe I am very powerful." Again I would watch the nervous glances and clear discomfort, as most people believed they had no power or they were not willing to discuss the topic at all. It was as if to discuss or admit to having any power would be an admission of desire to rule and control others. My final statement was always, "If you are not comfortable with power, you are most likely to abuse it. Great leaders use their power effectively." From that statement I would always open a discussion on power that I would keep alive during my stay at that organization. I believe my ability to create healthy, cohesive teams was directly related to my ability to have each team member take full responsibility for the power their position gave them and the power dynamics created as a result.

I believe you have an understanding of power when you are clear on what you are able to influence, as well as when you are able to distinguish between power, force and coercion. Here are some distinctions I have learned to use to assist me in maintaining clarity. As we look at each distinction, please refrain from looking from the point of view of good or bad; rather, look to understand and create clarity. As you lead, you will find each power position valuable; the question is when and how to use it.

> *Do you use Positional Power?*

This type of power is external and often granted through position, title or rank. This type of power gives a perception of effective leadership, however, one's ability to get people to act is often due to a perceived potential of loss or reward. Positional power, or using the power you have over an individual, most often allows you to manage rather that lead. I once had a boss who frequently reminded her staff the she was the executive director. She led by using threats, force and coercion. Although staff did what she requested, they disliked her and had little respect for her. They acted out of a fear of losing employment rather than from the inspired action that is the hallmark of an influential leader. Morale was most often low, staff underperformed and staff turnover was high.

I also worked for a boss that rarely used the power that came with her title. Instead, she led by example, invited open communication, and valued staff input. The work environment was dynamic, innovative and fun. Individuals often went above and beyond, taking pride in their ability to contribute to a larger outcome. Although this executive director clearly had the power of title and position, she rarely chose to wield it. Positional power was used when all other options had been exhausted or it was a situation where the team's input was not appropriate.

> *Have you chosen to underuse your*
> *power or be passive?*

I have also worked with leaders who had a strong desire to be liked, fearing repercussions for any decision they might make. Although they wanted to lead, they did not like the responsibility that came with the position. These leaders were easily influenced and their beliefs and values seemed to change from one event to another. Leaders in this category often used manipulation, coercion and presented themselves as powerless or the victim of circumstances. Team members did not respect these leaders and would rarely do what was requested.

Similarly, I have seen great leaders under use their power to enable someone to recover from a situation or save face. Although they could easily point out a wrongdoing and use their positional power to punish or set an example, they instead might identify a problem and create a space or circumstance that enables a person to save face and recover from a situation. This use of one's power will enhance the level of trust and create an environment where individuals are willing to take risks as well as admit errors.

> *Are you aware of your internal power?*

In my opinion, internal power is true power and the source of great leadership. Access to internal power comes from an understanding and a willingness to take responsibly for what one has influence over. This power is not dictated by events, circumstances or position. This power comes from within and is gained through confidence and the esteem one acquires from creating successful outcomes and overcoming challenges. Decisions are not made to seek approval or prove one's worth. Decisions and the use of power are guided by clear principles and values rather than by events and emotions. This leader's commitment is to equitable treatment and a larger vision, philosophy or process. Leaders who move from a primary space of internal power know that a desire to control external circumstances does not determine their value or effectiveness as a leader. As a result, they will use positional power or under use their power as a means to a very specific end. Leaders who are guided by internal power are respected for who they are as well as what they are able to achieve. For these leaders, the process is equally as important as the outcome.

> *The power we cultivate within us is the one*
> *form of power no one can take away.*

As important as it is to understand the different types of power positions, it is even more important not to limit yourself to one of these leadership styles. Knowing when to draw qualities from each position will produce the most successful and productive teams; however, focusing on developing your internal power is what can transform a great leader into an outstanding one. From great internal power comes an unparalleled sense of self-assurance, because if all else fails, the power we have inside us is what we are left with. Above all, the power we cultivate within us is the one form of power no one can take away.

Moving From Good to Great:

1. Where have you effectively managed the dynamics related to power in your life and business?
2. What has been the impact of your effective use of your power?
3. Where might you have overused your power or underused your power?
4. What was the impact of your actions?
5. How could you better exercise your power moving forward?
6. How will this change in behavior impact your life/business?

16. Attitude of Gratitude:

Vision + Faith + Courage + Solution Focus

> **I am grateful because I exist.**

I walk with the understanding that all is perfect right now. I have an appreciation for everything, whether I perceive it to be positive or negative. Gratitude is actually very simple: it is to understand the blessing of your existence. It is to stop and appreciate all the wonders of nature, or the miracle of life sung in the cry of a baby. It is to dance, appreciating your two left feet, or to savor the smell of your favorite food.

> *It is to be grateful for each small step.*

Many of you have blown the doors off your business or projects and have arrived in a brand new place. In times of great success, it is easy to be grateful. However, to understand gratitude is to celebrate your accomplishments, however large or small. It is to know that your gratitude for each small step is what will eventually compound into a magnificent mountain of success. It is to take the time to stop and give thanks to the small gift that will provide you with the stamina and endurance to eventually experience the large windfall. Gratitude is energy. To have gratitude is to use the blessings in your life as a fuel to propel you forward. Gratitude reminds us to be humble. It keeps us grounded and centered at times when success may be fueling our ego. Gratitude allows us to take the focus off of self and place it on someone else.

> *Gratitude pulls you into the present.*

Some of you may be far behind where you wanted to be. For some of you, very little has happened. In these times, gratitude is most important. Remembering to be grateful for the air you breathe, your health, or the liberty of self-expression is what will move you when things may not be working. Oprah Winfrey says, "The single greatest thing you can do to change your life today would be to start being grateful for what you have right now." You see, to be grateful pulls you into the present, the now, allowing you to focus on what is blessing your life in the moment. To have gratitude prevents us from running into the future, consuming our thoughts with worry about what has not yet occurred. Gratitude also prevents us from dwelling on the past, lingering in the land of regret, guilt, shame and blame. Sitting in the place of gratitude helps us to be mindful and present to our own growth and expansion, allowing us to take inventory of our resources and move forward.

> *To embody gratitude is to embrace*
> *all its ups and downs.*

Over the course of my journey, I've been in all those places. I've given it my all and still fell far short of my target. There have been years when I felt like there had been no growth at all. I have also had years when things were rocking and rolling and I doubled my income. I am grateful for it all. What has allowed me to keep going in spite of the ups and downs is faith and gratitude.

Know that growth does not occur without conflict and chaos. So be grateful! Every breakdown holds within it the promise of a breakthrough. To sit in gratitude is to learn to ask "What's great about this situation?" or "What am I supposed to learn?" It is to look for the blessing or solution when it is not apparent. I am reminded of all the conflict and all the breakdowns I've had the privilege of experiencing because through it all I have grown and become closer to my goals. To embody gratitude is to embrace all its ups and downs, twists and turns, even the potholes along the journey. As Melodie Beattie says, "Gratitude turns problems into gifts, failures into success, the unexpected into perfect timing, and mistakes into important events. Gratitude makes sense of our past, brings peace for today and creates a vision for tomorrow." What are you grateful for?

Moving From Good to Great:

1. What are you grateful for at this moment?
2. What impact has gratitude had in your life and business?
3. What new areas could you choose to be grateful for?
4. How will sitting in gratitude change or impact your life/business?

17. Learner:

(Knowledge + Action + Insight) x Time

> *I have a commitment to personal development and ongoing growth. I am coachable and open to new ideas and ways of being*

At an event I attended, international speaker and network marketing trainer Michael Clouse asked the audience if they had read the book *The Seven Habits of Highly Effective People* by Stephen Covey. Several people in the room raised their hands. He then asked how many could recite the seven habits. I am not sure if one person in the audience raised their hand. The question stuck with me, as I was one of the people who had read the book. To magnify the impact of Mr. Clouse's question, I had been featured on Steven Covey's CD *The Seven Habits of Highly Effective Network Marketers*, yet I could only remember one of the habits, the one I was asked to study and write about, the key words being "study and write."

> *Can you recite the Seven habits?*

The point Michel Clouse was clearly making was that leaders are learners. They read not only to acquire knowledge, but to acquire mastery. You see, most of us read because we have been taught that knowledge is power. We can recite theories, formulas and quotes, however, such recitation is often merely academic. The question is whether knowledge is truly power. World-renowned author Napoleon Hill says, "It is nothing of the sort! Knowledge is only potential power. It becomes power only, when, and if it is organized into definite plans of action and directed to a definite end." In other words, knowledge only becomes power when it moves from academia or theory into action and experience. It becomes power when we are willing to execute a plan, experience failure and have the courage to course-correct. It is power when it is used to achieve a worthy outcome.

> *Is knowledge truly power?*

How many books have you read? How many hours have you spent watching and listening to tapes, videos or CDs? How many weekends have you spent attending trainings and seminars? We participate in personal development activities all the time, but often we do so without acquiring mastery. To acquire mastery is to take the principles and knowledge, organize it into a definite plan, and live into it. I now believe we should read and re-read the books until we have integrated the principles into our daily habits of living. We must practice the principles and exemplify the skills, attitudes and behaviors that we believe we require in our business and lives.

> *Where do you need to gain mastery?*
> *What habits must you master?*

Inspired by the provocative question asked by Michael Clouse, I decided to not only re-read *The Seven Habits of Highly Effective People*, but to study and apply the habits. This endeavor was transformational. As I took the time to pull each habit into my life, I gained new insights, changed behaviors, and acquired new skills. I was no longer passive as I read each chapter; rather than practice cerebral gymnastics, I became active, creating a physical and cellular experience: creating true learning.

Network marketing is a perfect example of learning. Most people leave the profession before they even begin, calling it a scheme where only those at the top make the money. The reality is many fail because they do not give time for learning to occur. Like any other profession, there are skills and techniques unique to the profession of network marketing and one must be willing to put in the 10,000 hours required to truly master any craft. Unfortunately, many come to this fine profession with unrealistic expectations, expecting quick windfalls. The truth is they see the glory of those who have achieved success; however, they have not stopped to ask for the story, the story of those who have experienced past failure and disappointment followed by hours of workshops, CDs and books. The agony caused by not knowing who to call and how to prospect and present. The story of overcoming the fear of presenting to a group for the first time, followed by the experience of doing the presentation and no one showing up. To learn is to experience growth and mastery. It is to be willing to move from not-so-good to great.

Bonus 3: To assist on your journey to mastery, we have put together a monthly mentoring email, a short video and coaching questions designed to have you pull your new learning into your life. Go to www.lwcbook.com and register to receive your video series.

Moving From Good to Great:

1. Where have you applied the knowledge you have gained and experienced true learning?
2. How has this learning impacted your life and business?
3. Where might you be required to gain new knowledge and apply the lessons learned?
4. What can you do to acquire this new knowledge?
5. How will this new learning impact your life/business?

18. Self-Mastery:

(Organization + Positive Energy + Schedule) x Time

I am disciplined, organized, punctual and focused.

To have self-mastery is to have personal discipline. It is to manage our energy, actions and emotional state. It is to be punctual, respect deadlines and to maintain an orderly environment. *Webster's Dictionary* defines self-mastery as "the attainment of eminent skill or power." I believe it is to have the discipline to bring your best to all you choose to do.

The act of having personal mastery is to be present, giving 100% to who you are with and all you choose to do. It is to choose to play when it is time to play and to produce powerful outcomes when it is time to produce. To create self-mastery, one must first create a clearing. A clearing is the space available when we choose to remove all unnecessary clutter, actions and conversations, filling the space with only those activities that propel your life and business forward. I believe that to create true success and move toward our dreams, we must create a clearing in three key areas of our life. We must create a physical clearing, an emotional clearing, and a clearing in time.

Do you have a physical clearing?

I heard a multi-millionaire say that he could tell a leader by taking a look in the trunk of their car. I imagine as you read this, you're taking a quick mental inventory of the trunk of your car. Does the trunk of your car contain everything but the kitchen sink, or is it clean and tidy? Can you offer someone a ride without throwing books and CDs in the back seat and cleaning trash off the floor? Are you comfortable with guests dropping by your home unannounced? What about your office space? Do you have stacks of papers and books piled high on your desk or on the floor? Do you have a place for everything, and is everything in its place? Are your files in piles, or filed away neatly in your file cabinet? Are there sticky notes in disarray plastered everywhere? Are your guiding principles and dreams clear on a vision board?

Your physical space is a reflection of your inner mindset. It reflects your way of being, your level of inner peace. Your environment reflects your personal clarity or lack thereof. It mirrors your level of discipline and the organization of your thoughts and actions. Your physical environment exemplifies your mastery of self. I often can tell my mental state by looking at the state of my desk. If my desk is cluttered and disarrayed, it is often a signal for me to stop, breathe, clear out the clutter both physically and mentally and begin again. What is your physical space saying about you?

> *Do you have an emotional clearing?*

In addition to creating a clearing in space, we must also create an emotional clearing. They say, "Garbage in, garbage out." I have also heard that garbage in stays and pollutes. How are you nurturing your mind? What types of movies do you watch? What books do you read? In what types of activities do you engage? Who are the people with whom you spend the most time? Are you surrounded by people who inspire and motivate, or by naysayers that criticize and scoff at your dreams? Are you spending time with people that will move you forward, or people who will keep you cemented to your old ways of being? Do you surround yourself with individuals who know more than you in various areas of expertise, or are you the smartest one in your circle?

True leaders are discerning. They eliminate negative influences, selecting coaches, books, CDs and activities that nourish and build them intellectually, emotionally and spiritually. Leaders surround themselves with mentors who will assist them in areas required for their growth. They develop relationships with individuals that challenge them and make them stretch. When I began my journey, I had to take an inventory of who I was spending my time with. I soon realized the people surrounding me were a reflection of the life I desired to change: one full of debt, worry and a future of chasing someone else's cheese. I knew in order to get where I desired I would have to create my "Love Posse." A circle of influence filled with people who believed in my dreams. People who already had achieve what I desired. Who is in your Love Posse?

Do you have a clearing in time?

Once we have established a physical and emotional clearing, we must focus on a clearing in time. I believe structure creates freedom. What better way to create a space in time than through a schedule? A schedule assists us to create the space for everything and everyone important in our lives. Once we have created a clearing in time, we can devise an action plan for getting things accomplished and reaching our goals. Remember: what get scheduled gets done. This is where our power lies. The idea here is to synchronize and integrate your action plan with your schedule, your clearing in time.

As entrepreneurs and leaders, we must master ourselves in time. Masters know what they are doing from the beginning of the day till the end. Honoring your schedule allows you to move from busy to productive. It allows you to determine "how much by when." Adhering to a schedule says to the world, "I value my time. I understand that my time is my most valuable commodity, a currency more precious than money." A schedule affords us the freedom to say, "No, not now" without guilt, and come one hundred percent to everything we do. Honoring our schedule also teaches others to respect our enterprise and our time, knowing that the time we have allotted for them will be sacred and free of distraction.

When I began my first business, one of my mentors asked me to put a dollar value on my time. He advised me that my time was the most important asset I posses and I should use it wisely. He also told me that my dollar value should reflect where I was going, not where I had been. Being $50,000 upside down in credit card debt with a salary where there was more month than money, I gave my time a $150.00-per-hour value. My mentor then suggested that I eliminate from my schedule all activities that did not move me forward financially. He suggested I hold on to activities that could only be performed by me. The first thought that reared its head was the ever present "I don't have the money" conversation, meaning I couldn't afford to hire someone. He reminded me that if my mind said I could not afford it then I would never be able to afford it. He recommended I become creative and that success would be mine when I created the clearing in my life to produce the outcomes I desired. That year I learned to delegate, engaging grandparents to help with carpools and my sons to do many of the family chores. Payment was immense gratitude and allowance for the boys. I hired a housekeeper and contracted or bartered most of my office work. This small shift freed up fifteen hours in my week and created the foundation that allowed me to eventually leave my job.

Take a moment to reflect on your clearings: your physical, emotional and time spaces. What do these areas say about you and your state of mind? Does your office reflect your goals, dreams and vision? Or is your space indicative of a life of chaos and disarray you'd like to leave behind? Does your home and office reflect peace and clarity, or overwhelm and frustration? Is your circle of friends and family pulling you toward or pushing you away from your goals and aspirations? Are you surrounding yourself with people who challenge you to be more and encourage you to stretch? Do you honor your schedule and teach others to respect your time? Have you created time for the things and people you value? Take action to create your clearing, and develop habits that will maintain the space. Become a master of self in every aspect of your life, and your dreams will become your reality.

Moving from good to great:

1. What areas have you created a clearing in? (physical, emotional and time)
2. What impact have these clearings had in your life and business?
3. How might you improve your physical clearing?
4. How might you improve your emotional clearing?
5. How might you improve your clearing in time?
6. How will this new level of personal mastery impact your life/business?

19. Communication:

(Knowledge + Opinions + Facts) x Self Expression

> *I am fully self-expressed. I have an awareness of how to give and receive information for positive outcomes.*

What is communication? When I ask this question, the most common responses are: "speaking clearly," "active listening," "body language" and "using 'I' language." While those responses are correct, they only relate to the skill sets associated with active communication. I believe that how we communicate is a byproduct of all our experiences, values and beliefs. In other words, the perceptions we have about our past or future, influence how we communicate in the present. Our thoughts about ourselves and others shape our responses and how effectively we communicate. Have you ever been in a situation where you have reacted to an event or statement, and found yourself wondering "Where on Earth did that response come from?" The reality is that you were not responding at all. Rather, you were reacting. Your communication in that moment was triggered by the emotion left from some forgotten occurrence in your past.

> *We can choose to create a great day or a bad day.*

Think of a day where you looked in the mirror and did not like how you looked. Maybe someone made a negative comment to you, or an appointment you were counting on fell through. How did you react? In the past when this would occur, my energy would shift and I would begin to magnify every flaw or physical imperfection. Unconsciously, my internal negative dialogue would begin as I pulled the emotion from similar past events smack into my present. From that negative space my energy would continue to plummet, and suddenly my confidence and competence would begin a downward spiral. I would walk through the world looking to others to affirm my worth. I would live in my head, absorbed in my own negative self-talk, and unknowingly project myself as disconnected and unapproachable. The result would inevitably be that my inner world would influence my outer world. I would have a bad day.

Now remember a day when you stood in the mirror and said, "I look great!" Someone paid you a compliment, or a client you had been calling finally agreed to an appointment. This is the day where everything you desire shows up. On these days, I know my energy is up, as is my confidence and my sense of competence. I know that when the dialogue in my head is empowering and positive, I am instantly more attractive. I am present, living in the now, responding to the world with confidence and grace. I affirm myself. These are the days I walk into a room and live as though the world is *my* oyster. Again, my inner world creates my outer world and I have a great day.

In the movie *The Secret*, it is said that our thoughts become things, or what you think about, you bring about. Well, when looking at communication, our thoughts and perceptions, positive or negative, create our feelings and shape how effectively we communicate in the world. Our internal communication shapes or creates our external outcomes. To have powerful communication is to have command over your internal dialogue. It is to be able to change your thoughts from negative to positive in a moment. I remember being at a seminar and hearing the instructor say, "Some of you are the light and some of you are waiting for someone to shine a light on you." This struck me because at that point in my life I definitely was not the light. I was absorbed in negative self-talk and pity. I lacked confidence and looked to others to validate my worth.

> *So what creates you as the light?*

It is your internal dialogue. The communication you have with yourself. For a very small number of people, the positive self-talk that creates a positive self-esteem comes naturally. For most, it is a learned skill: an art that can only be developed through self awareness and practice. It requires mastery over one's internal dialogue and learning to respond rather than react. When such mastery exists, one communicates from a place of internal power versus a defensive place based in fear. Listening to the instructor talk about each of us being the light, trusting and generating from the energy and power that lives within, I recognized my need to do my own internal work; work that would allow me to rekindle the light I knew lived within.

> *What past events shape your communication?*

My earliest recollection of a memory that formed most

of my communication patterns occurred when I was six. I had an embarrassing event in grade one that for the longest time shaped my communication. I was asked to come to the front of the room and read. At that time, I still had my very Caribbean accent, and as I read, the teacher proceeded to correct how I enunciated every word. The class giggled, and what was actually a few short minutes seemed like hours. Well, in that moment I decided a few things about myself. I decided that I was not very smart and that I would never volunteer to speak in front of the room ever again. I actually went through school never raising my hand or asking for help.

As an adult, my communication was fine in small settings. If asked to answer a question in a large room or speak in front of a crowd, I would subconsciously be thrown back to my grade one event. I would react by becoming defensive. I would speak quickly, lose focus, and speak in broken and incoherent sentences. My heart would pound as I surrendered all my power to a past event, reinforcing my already negative self-talk and the belief that I could not communicate clearly, and that I was not smart or articulate.

It was not until I began to revisit past events, understand their impact in my present, and clear the emotion attached to the events, that I was able to move from reacting to responding. As I regained my power, I began to communicate effectively for the first time. You see, through my process of self-reflection, I realized the event in grade one had subconsciously left me fearful and anxious. The reality was that I would avoid any situation that could possibly recreate the feeling of embarrassment and shame I faced as a young child. Although the event was in the past, I was left powerless in my present by lingering emotions. I allowed myself to live in the shadow of others, never truly speaking my mind, never allowing myself the freedom to be fully self-expressed.

Become the light and trust your greatness.

Change came when I was willing to admit that the event had passed and the chatter in my head was the unresolved emotion. Change came when I was willing to admit that I had been walking with the belief that to risk being fully self-expressed would only result in pain and humiliation. I now had to change my internal dialogue. I had to become the light and trust the greatness I knew lived within me and act accordingly. I had to create a new belief.

Today, I am fully self expressed. I am able to speak in front of thousands of people. I believe my biggest gift to my audience is my willingness to be vulnerable. Each time I take the stage, I reinforce my new belief that I have brilliance within me and my responsibility is to share my gift with the world. I invite you to live boldly, communicate powerfully, and share your gifts with the world.

Moving From Good to Great:

1. Where is your communication effective and where are you fully self expressed?
2. How does this communication impact your life and business?
3. Where and with whom might you be required to improve your communication?
4. What internal dialogue will you be required to shift to improve your communication in this area?
5. What impact will this improved communication have on your life/business?

20. Conflict:

Opinion + Opposition

I am comfortable with disagreement and different or opposing viewpoints. I welcome healthy debates and view them as an opportunity for growth.

Have you ever considered what it would be like to be a powerful communicator in all situations? Wouldn't it be wonderful to have the mastery to respond rather than react during the most challenging of circumstances? This is what is available when you begin to embrace conflict. When you hear the word "conflict," what comes to mind? I viewed conflict as stressful, bad and unpleasant. Conflict was something I should avoid. My historical experience of conflict taught me that conflict was always scary, and the person who was the strongest, loudest or most intimidating won the battle.

As I became an adult, I utilized silence and withdrawal as my primary tool for managing conflict. I walked through the world suppressed and angered by wrongdoings. I became resentful of any difference of opinion because I was unwilling to express my own. My limited view of conflict caused me to leave many events in my life unresolved. I shoved them under the proverbial carpet and walked around frustrated, wondering why I did not receive the respect I believed I deserved.

I changed my view of conflict.

My access to empowered communication came when I chose to change my view of conflict. Conflict can be external or internal. External conflict is a difference of opinion or points of view between two or more people, two opposing ideas bumping into one another. It can be antagonistic, but not necessarily a negative experience.

Conflict occurs internally when we experience turmoil because our beliefs or values are being challenged, or when we are faced with a moral questions or decisions. Unfortunately, we are socialized to see conflict as a negative thing. The reality is you cannot live in the world without conflict. Conflict is the catalyst for change and growth for yourself and the world. When you begin to see conflict as a precursor for change, then it becomes part of a natural process of development.

You can approach conflict as an opportunity to grow. You can view it as an event that is actually creating a shift for yourself and others. Embracing conflict allows you to become solution focused, and in the process you understand that the discomfort you experience in the moment is life saying it is time for change. Conflict provides access to your greatness and empowerment. Change is rarely comfortable, but it can provide a clearing for you to move from good to great.

Choose Your Battles

My access to empowered communication further expanded when I was able to distinguish the difference between conflict and confrontation. This one distinction enabled me to understand it was my responsibility to choose how I handled situations where there were opposing views, values and beliefs. I learned to relinquish the belief that things happen *to me,* and embrace the belief that things occur *through me.* I had the power to initiate or close down most challenging situations.

To confront is the action of doing something about a conflict. It is to initiate and welcome the dialogue necessary for conflict resolution. It is to choose to intervene and create change. A conflict is an experience, while confrontation is the act of doing something about the experience.

Once I made this distinction, I became aware of how frequently conflict occurs in a day. I have an opinion and someone else has a totally different opinion. I have a desire to take a specific action and someone else desires another action. How many times in the day do you come to a crossroad where there are two opposing opinions or points of view? I realized conflict when I perceived loss, or when agreeing with an opposite point of view would compromise one of my values or put me at a disadvantage. I noticed a conflict when I felt I was required to give up something I valued. I would often become defensive and either confront or retreat. I would react, often subconsciously, collapsing conflict and confrontation as one.

Understanding the distinction between conflict and confrontation enabled me to stop, define the perceived conflict, and assess how or if I desired to respond. Learning to choose to respond has allowed me to choose my battles, avoid unnecessary chaos, and take responsibility for how I interact with those around me.

Here are eight questions I use to define a conflict and determine how I choose to respond. Usually by the time I get to questions 3 and 4, I realize my desire to confront is actually a desire to control. When I choose to move through all the steps and confront, I am clear, respectful and willing to take full responsibility for the outcome.

1. What is the conflict?
2. How am I feeling?
3. What is my perceived loss and what is the cost?
4. How can I understand the other person's point of view?
5. Is there an easy win – win?
6. What is my purpose for confronting?
7. What outcome am I seeking?
8. How can I confront respectfully?

Moving From Good to Great:

1. Where in your life and business are you effective at dealing with conflict?
2. How does your present method of dealing with conflict impact your life/business?
3. Where could you become more effective at dealing with conflict?
4. What will you be required to change to improve your method of dealing with conflict?
5. What impact will your improved method of dealing with conflict have on your life/business?

Conclusion

You have just reviewed twenty habits of highly successful business leaders. Now it is time to ensure you understand the power that comes with consistently applying each habit. Jeff Olson calls it "the Slight Edge." Darren Hardy, the publisher of *Success* magazine, calls it the Compound Effect. He states that any behavior compounded over time will create momentum. It is now important to create the mindset or context that will have you understand the impact of consistent repetition.

I remember having dinner with a gentleman who spoke to me about a conspiracy theory. He explained that the families who have the power in our nation for generations have groomed their children to assume power when they became adults. The 1% of the world that held the majority power had systematically taught their children habits and a mindset to ensure their family would maintain a monopoly on the market. His conspiracy theory was actually the Compound Effect: consistent grooming compounded over generations.

As I listened, I was intrigued and admittedly amused by his position. I could not help but ask myself if it was only the wealthy that groomed their children. I have come to believe we are all groomed by our parents and environment. The question is, what are we being groomed for? Are we being groomed for success, or are we being groomed for failure? Is our grooming preparing us for a wealth mindset, or is our grooming preparing us for a poverty mindset?

> *All parents have their own conspiracy theory.*

All parents have their own conspiracy theory, a plan or agreement that is passed on from one generation to another. This plan consists of habits, beliefs and actions that are instilled into the next generation, creating a mindset which attracts a certain outcome. The difference is that 80% of the population's plan occurs by default, while those who create wealth or success have a plan by design. Universal principles remain the same whether you are wealthy or poor. What you consistently repeat over time creates conditioning, and those habits create your results. The question then becomes are your habits, moving you closer to wealth or further away. We label the actions of the wealthy a "conspiracy theory" or a secret plan because so few amongst us understand the need to systematically plan for success, and so few of us understand that it is the compound effect of our habits and mindset that creates wealth.

The reality is whether a plan is for poverty or success, it is what you believe and focus on that will determine your results. Once an intention is set and habits are consistently applied, one will most like achieve the results you expect. The key is to examine your beliefs and expectations. Do they have you focus on the results you desire? Or are your beliefs and expectations unknowingly pulling your energy in a completely different direction. Next, examine your habits. Will your habits move you towards your goals or pull you further away? While it may be easier for those who have been groomed by parents and families who already have success to recreate success, success is not a conspiracy theory reserved for a secret group. It is a formula that can be learned by those who truly desire more.

As I continued to listen to this gentleman speak, I was struck by the time and energy he had spent researching the habits and actions of those who create wealth. My confusion led me to search to understand why he would study their actions yet not model them and change the direction of his life. What became evident was a common error. This gentleman was unable to distinguish between habits and intention. He disagreed with the mission of the wealthy "to keep the wealth in the hands of the 1%." As a result, he failed to look further and learn from the behaviors that consistently allowed them to recreate their wealth.

> *Model the habits of someone who you*
> *would like to trade places with.*

Think of two highly successful people: one you admire and one you believe might be self-serving and less than honorable. Now examine their habits. Chances are you will see two people with exceptional personal mastery. You see, I am not asking whether you agree with their mission, goal or purpose; I am asking you to study their daily habits. Whether their intent is honorable or malicious, a person who consistently applies a series of habits which in turn reinforce a preexisting mindset will eventually have success. Oprah is a woman I greatly admire. Her habits and mindset are among those I have chosen to model. The reality is, if Oprah had chosen to use her gifts for evil, with her habits and mindset, she would most likely have achieved her goals and become a force to be reckoned with. The world is blessed by Oprah's mission and purpose, which is to serve and uplift others. It is not the habits one must question; it is the intention that drives each habit. While habits are a product of grooming, what motivates intention is determined by the love and peace within our hearts. If success and wealth are what you truly desire, select two successful people you truly admire, study their lifestyle, habits and mindset.

Bonus 4: Go to www.lwcbook.com and listen to **Mentoring with Millionaires.** Learn from the successful business minds that have inspired my growth and success.

Time for action!

Knowledge without action is just an exercise in mental gymnastics. It has no lasting impact in your life. This book is designed to create change, to help you find the leader that already lives within you and attract the life you truly deserve. Once you have studied the habits and mindset of your two successful people, begin to model them. Each month, select the habits that will allow you to create the change that is most needed in your life. Use the working definitions to inspire the action which will serve you most. Remember, words create pictures, pictures elicit emotions, and emotions create our actions.

Sam is the father of two amazing boys. Sam's highest priority was to provide for his boys and ensure they had all the resources they required to succeed. Like many men, Sam's primary focus was creating the income his family needed. Sam worked long hours, which at times would have him miss commitments with his sons and family. While friends would say Sam did not honor his commitments, "commitment" was not the word from the Penthouse Leadership Assessment that inspired him to change. In Sam's mind, he was very committed to his family; in his mind, every action and the long hours he worked were a reflection of his commitment. The word that inspired Sam was "integrity." Sam realized he was not honoring his word with his sons. It had begun to impact their relationship, leaving his sons feeling unimportant. This was the complete opposite of Sam's intent. Committed to change, Sam began to work to restore his integrity, setting aside family time with his sons. His commitment was to show up on time, accept no business calls during their time together, and to make his sons his sole priority during the time he spent with them. After a few months, Sam had begun to restore his integrity with his sons. Sam's word became a declaration his sons could count on. Sam realized integrity was crucial, as it made his commitment to his sons a real experience in each of their lives.

The final step is to build and execute a plan. Track your progress by going to www.lwcbook.com and revisit the Penthouse Leadership Assessment. Monitor your scores and course-correct until the habit becomes part of your automatic way of being. When your new habit begins to attract the results you are seeking, celebrate. Celebrate and share your success with others. Write your testimonial and send it to the HartZone. The contribution of your testimonial will motivate others and become the inspiration for their success. Remember, the first person we each lead is ourselves. The cool thing is that the world is watching. Be the leader others desire to follow.

Go to www.hartzone.com and submit your testimonial.

My final request is for you to ignite the leader in someone else. Give them the gift of *Leading With*

Character. Recommend or give a copy of this book to five people in your life. The world requires that we all take the first step in leadership and lead ourselves.

1. _____

2. _____

3. _____

4. _____

5. _____

To order your copies of
Leading with Character visit
www.leadingwithcharacterbook.com.

www.ingramcontent.com/pod-product-compliance
Lightning Source LLC
Chambersburg PA
CBHW060615200326
41521CB00007B/777